ESSENTIAL
ART THERAPY
EXERCISES

ESSENTIAL ART THERAPY EXERCISES

EFFECTIVE TECHNIQUES TO MANAGE ANXIETY, DEPRESSION, AND PTSD

Leah Guzman, ATR-BC

ROCKRIDGE
PRESS

Interior and Cover Designer: Suzanne LaGasa

Art Producer: Tom Hood

Editor: Shannon Criss

Production Editor: Mia Moran

Images © Shutterstock/Azurhino cover; Shutterstock/S-BELOV p. vi; Shutterstock/Annie Brusnika p. vi; iStock/Alex_Wang1 pp. vi, 48; Shutterstock/Lu_Lova p. vi; Shutterstock/think4photop p. vi; Shutterstock/Irina Simkina p. vi; iStock/shoo_arts pp. vi, 41; Shutterstock/Cincinart p. vi; Shutterstock/Skolkokrasok p. vi; iStock/beastfromeast p. 21; Shutterstock/arxichtu4ki p. 24; iStock/Zinaida Kostiukovich p. 29; iStock/Marina Indova p. 61; iStock/Oleh_Slobodeniuk p. 67; iStock/Sasiistock p. 69; Shutterstock/Elena Ray pp. 74, 102; Shutterstock/FotoHelin p. 81; Shutterstock/anastasiya adamovich p. 83; Shutterstock/sutsaiy p. 85; iStock/PeopleImages p. 99; iStock/Rawpixel p. 117; iStock/amoklv p. 118; Shutterstock/Olesya Tseytlin p. 122; Shutterstock/Trinet Uzun p. 137; Shutterstock/Benjavisa Ruangvaree Art p. 140

Author photo courtesy of Leah Guzman

ISBN: Print 978-1-64611-162-6 | eBook 978-1-64611-163-3

R0

This book is dedicated to those who are suffering.
Let art be the tool that guides you on the path to recovery.

CONTENTS

INTRODUCTION

The intention of my art therapy practice is to create a safe place for clients to experience and creatively express their emotions, as well as to cultivate new opportunities for navigating life. Art has been an outlet for me during turbulent times, and it has been my first defense when dealing with life's challenges. Art is also a part of my daily regimen of keeping my life in balance. I practice what I preach. My mission is to support others in finding a way to connect body, mind, and soul through creativity. It's incredibly satisfying to help a person realize their true potential and live a life free of suffering. As a registered, board-certified art therapist (ATR-BC), I run a private practice that provides these services to all age groups, both in person and online. My experience with adolescent clients ranges from working with at-risk youth in crisis shelters and juvenile jails to kids in public schools. I also have vast experience working with adults who have anxiety, depression, and trauma. Outside of my private practice, I have also worked in psychiatric facilities and women's shelters.

My clinical experience has been using the cognitive-behavioral art therapy approach to treat depression, anxiety, and post-traumatic stress disorder (PTSD). Cognitive-behavioral approaches, including mindfulness practices and meditation, are also a part of my art therapy method. Art therapy is a way for clients to visualize what's going on in their mind and learn new ways to change their thinking patterns, which can lead to a new perspective. This book provides creative techniques for dealing with depression, anxiety, and PTSD. If you are a mental health professional, try the exercises yourself before doing them with your client. If you are doing these art exercises independently, give yourself time to reflect by journaling the discussion questions.

My hope is that this book will provide a springboard for insight, self-expression, mindfulness, acceptance, and self-compassion. Specifically, the exercises are designed to provide visual representations of thoughts and feelings. When people learn that they have control over their thoughts, and how they choose to feel, it will affect their behavior. Everyone can learn new ways to respond to situations in their lives. Art therapy isn't solely for people with an artistic disposition. It can also be helpful to those who consider themselves nonartistic. Anyone open to learning techniques that foster self-awareness can gain something from the experience.

Those who are new to creating art should focus on the process rather than the product. To accomplish this, they must let go of critical thoughts because judging whether artwork is good or bad will stop the creative process. The act of expression is what is valuable because it provides insight into emotions and behaviors. Creating art to express emotions can be truly cathartic and liberating. Everyone should take the time to loosen up by trying the warm-up exercises I've included at the end of chapter 1. When an individual is open to looking inward and finding new ways to cope with life events through creating art without judgment, transformation happens. The world begins to change. If thoughts of judgment come up, just witness them and do not respond. They are only thoughts. Keep the intention clear to use these exercises to heal and to learn new ways to exist comfortably in the world.

Part One

The Art of

Therapy

Chapter One

WHAT IS ART THERAPY?

ART THERAPY IS A PSYCHOTHERAPEUTIC APPROACH to treating emotional and behavioral disorders that uses art and psychology to help improve lives. Through the art-making process, participants can express their emotions and heal what is causing their anxiety, depression, or PTSD. Art therapists are master's-level clinicians trained to create therapeutic relationships with participants to facilitate opportunities that will improve cognition, self-awareness, and self-esteem, and increase coping and social skills. The art therapy exercises in this book include an array of techniques ranging from making collages and textiles to drawing, painting, sculpting, writing, and photography. The exercises relate specifically to treatment goals and emotional needs.

THE ORIGINS OF ART THERAPY

Art has always served as a way for humans to communicate. We can trace its origins to the first cave paintings discovered in Spain that date back thousands of years. The visual language of art still plays an important role in our daily lives. We are surrounded by images. Whether we're walking down the street and see a crossing signal, or we're navigating the Internet at home on the couch, art is everywhere. Art therapy is a helpful tool to make sense of the world around us.

According to an article titled "Art Therapy" on the GoodTherapy website, the origins of art therapy were first documented simultaneously in Europe and the United States in the 20th century. Adrian Hill, a British artist, author, and art therapist, first coined the phrase "art therapy" in 1942. In 1938, while Hill was being treated for tuberculosis in a sanatorium, he realized the therapeutic value of art for the sick. He began working with other patients at their bedsides and wrote a book called *Art Versus Illness*, which documents his discoveries.

The "Art Therapy" article also outlines additional contributors to the field. In the United States in early 1900, Margaret Naumburg—an American psychologist, educator, artist, author, and the so-called "mother of art therapy"—wrote about her experiences with psychotherapy and art. She wrote books alongside her contemporaries and sparked a movement to provide art therapy in schools, which led to the creation of university-level master's art therapy programs. Hanna Kwiatkowska, a talented artist who worked at the National Institute of Mental Health, assisted families in improving their dynamics through art therapy. Florence Cane, an art educator, proposed a process-oriented art-as-therapy approach that focuses on ego support, identity development, and self-growth improvement. Edith Kramer advanced the field by establishing the art therapy program at New York University, where she was also a professor. Elinor Ulman was the founder of *The American Journal of Art Therapy* at a time where no other publication of art therapy existed. Since the first writings about art therapy, the profession has grown and become widely accepted as an effective treatment modality found in a variety of settings. Technological advances have expanded the profession by creating access to information and exercises online. Today, we also use technology as a tool for healing.

WHY ART THERAPY?

The goal of art therapy is to use a creative process to gain self-awareness and self-reflection in order to gain personal insight and develop self-control over emotions. Artwork is a visual documentation of thoughts and feelings. These mental images can offer solutions to problems and insights into the cause of these feelings. These insights provide a starting point for accepting those feelings and learning how to create new responses to emotions. The long-term benefits of this process include improved self-esteem, richer self-empowerment, and the development of skills that can be used in the future to deal with life's challenges.

Research in the cognitive-behavioral art therapy (CBAT) field supports the benefits of art therapy. According to Marcia Rosal in her book *Cognitive Behavioral Art Therapy*, evidence-based research proves that the CBAT approach is the most effective treatment for anxiety, depression, and PTSD. The goal of CBAT is to teach an individual to adapt to different life situations by increasing coping skills and by learning how to adapt to the environment.

Art therapy can also increase self-esteem. Completing a piece of art can bring feelings of accomplishment, empowerment, and satisfaction to someone who is suffering from depression. By reflecting on the artwork created, and following the prompts in this book, insights into the unconscious mind can be gained.

Discussing the work also increases self-awareness. If someone is suffering from depression or anxiety, looking at the artwork and discussing it leads to self-reflection, which improves self-awareness and increases self-control. Having more control over emotions leads to emotional resilience. Emotional resilience is the awareness of thoughts and what drives those thoughts. A person who is emotionally resilient has self-regulation and is able to cope with stressful situations. Self-regulation is about choosing constructive ways to manage feelings as they arise, rather than destructive ways that often lead to regret. Learning how to take charge of your feelings leads to healing.

Art therapy can help identify what causes emotional stress and develop constructive engagement for dealing with it. For example, someone suffering from PTSD will need to explore the triggers associated with their trauma. Creating art that recalls one's memory is a cognitive process. People suffering from PTSD need to engage with what caused the initial stress and work through their emotions. By exploring these emotions and integrating them into their psyche, the person is able to process the life experience to reconcile their trauma.

Art therapy also increases problem-solving abilities, as some exercises are designed to have you find alternative ways of handling situations. According to Rosal, as cognitive skills improve, problem-solving skills also improve. Rosal found that the creative process also enhances decision making. Throughout the art-making process you have many opportunities to make decisions when you choose colors, details, and layout.

Group art therapy is effective because it allows participants to practice communication as a part of the therapy process, which also increases socialization. My favorite part of group art therapy sessions is when individuals discuss the meaning of their work with other group members. When the participant shares their story, it gives other members an opportunity to know them on a more personal level. The other members provide support by listening, giving feedback, and providing suggestions. The process creates a sense of connectedness and community.

Physical Benefits of Art Therapy

Although art therapy has numerous benefits to mental health, it can have a positive effect on one's physiological welfare as well. Stress manifests itself into our physical bodies every day. Physical symptoms may show up as headaches, backaches, tight muscles, shoulder pain, nervous stomach, fatigue, high blood pressure, overeating, or insomnia. Learning how to identify what is causing stress and how to cope with it will lead to a healthier lifestyle.

According to a 2016 study by Girija Kaimal, art was shown to have a positive effect on participants' stress levels. In this study, participants had their stress hormone cortisol measured before they made any art. They then had their cortisol levels measured again after a 45-minute session of creating art. A comparison of results showed that 75 percent of the participants had decreased cortisol levels after the art session. The most interesting part of this study is that the participants didn't have any background or experience in creating art. The process of creating art helps you physically relieve stress, even when you don't realize it. In my practice, I find that most participants enjoy the process, yet have difficulty making time for it in their everyday lives.

ART AND THERAPY CONNECTION

There are two views of how art therapy can be used in sessions: "art as therapy" and "art in therapy." Art *as* therapy is considered product-oriented because it's satisfying to create a piece of art that is aesthetically pleasing. The act of producing the artwork is an end to itself. The creative process can foster self-awareness, boost self-esteem, and increase personal growth. For example, if I create a mug out of clay, the mug will make me feel good because I created it. Thus, my self-esteem increases.

The intention behind art *in* therapy is as a vehicle for psychotherapy to dig deeper into emotions and explore one's feelings and thoughts. To continue my mug metaphor: What does the mug represent to me? What feeling do I want to achieve? How will the mug be used to deal with anxiety? I can make a cup of tea when anxiety arises. This book will provide many techniques for art in therapy. Art is a symbolic language that taps into the unconscious. Process, form, content, and verbal associations impart understanding about what is happening in an individual's life. This approach helps resolve emotional conflicts, develop insight, and teach new skills that can be used to navigate life.

Art therapy is effective at treating anxiety, depression, and PTSD. According to the National Institute of Mental Health (NIMH), anxiety is a feeling that comes up in different areas of life, and often it's a healthy and expected result. It becomes a disorder when excessive worry interferes with relationships, or work, or school performance. CBAT teaches different ways of responding to anxiety-producing situations.

The NIMH defines depression as a severe mood disorder that affects daily activities for at least two weeks. Symptoms include sadness, irritability, feelings of guilt or worthlessness, appetite changes, difficulty sleeping (or excessive sleeping), decreased energy or fatigue, and thoughts of death or suicide. The

CBAT approach addresses thought patterns related to depressive symptoms. Medication management combined with art therapy has been determined to be the best approach to treatment.

PTSD, as defined by NIMH, is a disorder that some people develop after experiencing a shocking, scary, or dangerous event. It is natural to feel afraid during a traumatic situation. The fight-or-flight response is a typical reaction to protect us from harm. Most people recover naturally, but some people will continue to feel stressed or frightened when they are no longer in danger. The CBAT approach addresses the traumatic event through different media. This enables the individual to process the emotions so the past event no longer feels overwhelming.

Studies have also shown that when people practice gratitude through journaling, they feel less burnt out at work, they sleep better, and they heal faster from health problems. A study from UCLA's Mindfulness Awareness Research Center showed that gratitude promotes the function of gray matter in our brain, which has a positive effect on the central nervous system.

INTERPRETING THERAPY

Interpreting artwork involves understanding all aspects of the art, and it's important to be nonjudgmental in the process. Art is subjective, and each of us comes to it with our own projections. The most important part of reflecting on art is for the artist to verbalize their associations. For example, blue may be associated with sadness by one person, but represent a sense of freedom by another. Please note that professional therapists have extensive training and diligent clinical skills to provide a safe experience in creating and processing art. If questions or concerns arise when interpreting art, it is critical to involve or consult with a trained art therapist.

Whether in a group art therapy environment, or between client and therapist, an important first step is to ask questions before jumping to conclusions. Always ask open-ended questions to avoid projection or giving personal interpretations to artwork.

Below are examples of open-ended questions to consider. It's ideal to document responses for future reference. This can be accomplished by writing them in a journal or on the back of the art you've created.

Questions to consider when reviewing work:

- How would you describe the image objectively (lines, shapes, objects, colors used)?
- What feelings came up as you made the artwork?
- How would you describe part of the artwork using the word "I"?
- How do different parts of the artwork communicate with one another to make a cohesive piece?
- What do the colors mean to you?
- What title would you give your art? What is the thought process behind that title?
- How does this art relate to your life right now?
- If your art had a message for you, what would it say?

In addition, there are several visual indicators to consider when interpreting art. They include:

- Excessive erasures
- Use of space
- Relationship of objects
- Missing body parts
- Lack of hands or feet
- Marks on a body
- Line quality
- Lack of color
- Color associations

In the therapeutic relationship, it is necessary for the therapist to create a safe place for clients so they can build trust and open up about their feelings. Creating art can bring about heavy emotional responses and feelings of shame, guilt, sadness, anger, or apathy. A trained therapist will be able to navigate the session to encourage and support the participant to sublimate their feelings. If overwhelming feelings emerge while using this book, contact a trained therapist from the American Art Therapy Association website (arttherapy.org).

Guided Imagery

Guided imagery is a verbal narrative that can be used to evoke feelings or develop problem solving skills. Visualization can be used to evoke the feeling of relaxation or peace, or to manifest something in life. Visualization can also be a tool to investigate how to cope with current situations. Most visualizations are done by closing your eyes and imagining a scene, then drawing it out.

GETTING STARTED WITH ART THERAPY

There are certain factors to consider when starting art therapy. If you choose to meet with a trained art therapist, it's important to make a commitment to scheduling time for your self-care. Healing and self-awareness are processes of self-development that unfold with time. An art therapist will design treatment goals and exercises specifically to meet your healing needs. To practice any of the exercises in this book on your own, you will also need to consider your time, gather materials, claim a space for an art practice, warm up to creating, and choose an activity that resonates with you. I prefer to start my practice with a centering meditation to ground myself. This allows me to stay focused on my art.

Supplies

To start practicing art therapy, you will need a variety of nontoxic materials. For drawing, it's essential to have an assortment of pencils, colored pencils, oil pastels, charcoal, and colored markers. For painting, I prefer watercolors and acrylics since they dry quickly and are easy to clean up. I do not recommend oil paints. They take much longer to dry and can contain toxic additives. They also require solvents to clean up. Here's a complete list of items you'll need for the exercises in this book:

Drawing Tools

- Assorted markers
- Black pen
- Charcoal
- Colored pencils
- Drawing pencils
- Fabric markers
- Oil pastels

Paints

- Acrylics
- Fabric paint
- Paint pens
- Spray paint
- Watercolors

Paper

- Butcher paper
- Heavy-weight drawing paper
- Journal
- Magazines
- Poster board
- Tissue paper
- Tracing paper

Sculpting

- Alginate
- Aluminum foil
- Assorted wooden or cardboard boxes
- Ceramic bowl
- Cord
- Fabric
- Face mold
- Felt
- Found objects
- Gesso spray
- Mod Podge®
- Model Magic®
- Petroleum jelly
- Photographs
- Pillow stuffing
- Plaster wrap
- Polymer clay
- Sculpting tools
- Self-drying clay
- Tin mint box
- Wire

Accessories

- Blow-dryer
- Computer (a tablet, laptop, or a desktop will work for most applications)
- Cup of water
- Erasers
- Glue stick
- Hammer
- Hot glue gun and glue sticks
- Liquid glue
- Masking tape
- Paintbrushes
- Plastic bags (small and large)
- Printer
- Scissors
- Sewing machine (optional)
- Sewing needles
- Smartphone
- Thread

HEALTHY HEALING PLACE

It's incredibly important to have a safe, inviting space for art therapy sessions. An ideal space is private, has a window for natural lighting, a nice table to work on, and a plethora of art materials. For a group setting, participants should sit in a circle around a large table to increase communication and cohesion of the group. The therapist should have all materials ready before starting the exercise. Keeping the materials in the middle of the table makes it easy to share. If practicing these exercises solo, find a place with limited distractions. Placing a "Do Not Disturb" sign in the space can be helpful.

If a person is doing the art exercises independently, I highly recommend a session with an art therapist to process the varied thoughts and emotions. The therapist will provide insight and reflection that might be difficult to see alone. Therapists may also offer online sessions as well as in-person appointments. When they do offer online sessions, they meet on a HIPPA-compliant platform, which means your session stays confidential.

WARM-UPS/MENTAL STRETCHING

The following warm-ups are a great way to loosen up and practice expression before starting a longer exercise. Sometimes people are intimidated by a blank sheet of paper. Warm-up exercises can break down this barrier and encourage the relaxation process. I recommend that at least one of these warm-ups be completed daily. By practicing healing rituals a few minutes each day people can learn new habits for promoting positive mental health.

Feeling Identification

Exercise time: 10 minutes
Benefit: Identifies and expresses feelings

MATERIALS: Paint pens, crayons, or markers (whichever you prefer); 1 sheet of 18-by-24-inch heavy-weight drawing paper

1. Choose a color that reflects how you're feeling today.
2. Draw a circle with that color.
3. In that circle, use lines and shapes to draw an image or images to identify how you're feeling today.
4. Name your art.

Breathing Through Lines

Exercise time: 10 minutes
Benefits: Raises awareness of breathing and assists in relaxation

MATERIALS:
Paintbrush, watercolors, 1 sheet of 18-by-24-inch heavy-weight drawing paper, cup of water

1. Wet your paintbrush and choose a color to add.
2. Take a deep breath in through your nose. Hold your breath while you place your brush in the upper-left corner of the paper. As you exhale slowly, draw a wavy line.
3. Choose either the same color or a different color (don't forget to rinse your brush if it's a different color) and add it to your paintbrush. Take a deep breath in as you place your brush on the paper. This time, as you exhale, make a large circle with one breath.
4. Choose a color, but this time take short breaths in and out. With each exhale, make quick marks or ticks on the paper.
5. Pick a final color and breathe in deeply. Choose your own mark or symbol to add as you exhale.

Favorite Song Drawing

Exercise time: 5 minutes
Benefit: Connects feelings to the act of drawing expressive lines

MATERIALS: Favorite song ready to be played aloud, colored pencils, 1 sheet of 18-by-24-inch heavy-weight drawing paper

Play your favorite song and use lines and color to express the melody you feel.

Scribble Into a Drawing

Exercise time: 10 minutes
Benefit: Taps into unconscious desires or issues

MATERIALS: Oil pastels, 1 sheet of 18-by-24-inch heavy-weight drawing paper, colored pencils

1. Close your eyes and, with an oil pastel, draw a scribbled line on the paper.

2. Look at your scribble from different angles. Observe the length and texture.

3. Create an image out of your scribble using the colored pencils.

What's Your Name?

Exercise time: 10 minutes
Benefits: Fosters expression and increases self-esteem

MATERIALS: Assorted markers, 1 sheet of 18-by-24-inch heavy-weight drawing paper

1. Using block letters, write your name in any color on your paper from left to right.

2. Think of a positive word that has the same first letter as your name. Add this word to your drawing in any location on the paper.

3. Pick your favorite colors and create a design inside the letters of your name.

Expressive Free Flow

Exercise time: 10 minutes
Benefit: Moves the body in large ways to loosen up and become expressive

MATERIALS: Masking tape, large sheet of butcher paper, assorted markers

1. Using the masking tape, hang a large sheet of butcher block paper on your wall.

2. While standing, hold a marker of any color and move your arm in a large circle to draw on the paper.

3. Continue to create many large circles on your paper using different colors. Be sure to alternate arms.

Centering Meditation

Exercise time: 5 minutes
Benefits: Teaches meditation, fosters relaxation, slows down an active brain, and pulls focus to the present moment

MATERIALS: Phone or computer to play the Centering Meditation from leahguzman.com /centering-meditation

1. Sit in a comfortable spot and hit play on the meditation recording.
2. Once it starts playing, follow the meditation process.
3. Repeat this breathing exercise 3 times. If any thoughts come up, simply observe them and let them go.

Gratitude Check-In

Exercise time: 5 minutes
Benefit: Increases positive effects on the nervous system

MATERIALS:
Journal, pen

In your journal, list five things that happened today for which you are grateful. This exercise can be done daily, either when you wake up or going to bed.

Power Affirmation

Exercise time: 10 minutes
Benefits: Creates a positive mindset and identifies real life events that support your affirmations

MATERIALS: Pencil, 1 sheet of 18-by-24-inch heavy-weight drawing paper, assorted markers

1. With your pencil, write an affirmation on the paper using bubble or block letters. An affirmation is a positive and short statement designed to help in goal manifestation. The key is to frame it as a confirmation of something that is true, even if you feel it's not quite true yet. Repeating an affirmation over and over will help it to become true.

   Examples of affirmations include:

   I am worthy.

   I'm learning that it's okay to make mistakes.

   I am open to discovering new meaning in life.

   I love and accept myself the way I am.

2. Choose a marker and trace over the message. Hang the message where you will see it daily. Every day, say the affirmation out loud with deep conviction. Positive thoughts generate positive feelings and attract positive life experiences.

Mindful Sketch

Exercise time: 10 minutes
Benefit: Increases mindfulness and focus in the moment

MATERIALS: Drawing pencil, 1 sheet of 18-by-24-inch heavy-weight drawing paper

Choose an object near you (such as a mug, plant, or book) and sketch out its shape. Add as many details as you like.

Part Two

Art of
Therapy
Exercises

Chapter Two

PAINTING AND DRAWING

DRAWING AND PAINTING ARE GREAT WAYS to tap into your creativity. Drawing with pencils and pens provides structure and control, while painting with a paint brush is fluid and loose. Both techniques can be used to express your emotions. Keep a sketchbook on hand to draw your surroundings, capture inspiring ideas, or document your feelings. It's a great way to keep track of your emotions and the stimuli that trigger those emotions.

Animal Guides

BENEFITS:

Increases self-awareness, develops emotional resilience, and assists in identifying individual strengths

Prep time:
10 minutes

Exercise time:
50 minutes

MATERIALS:

Drawing pencil

1 sheet of 18-by-24-inch heavy-weight drawing paper

Black pen

Colored pencils

Drawing animal images helps stimulate inspiration and comfort. But, most important, the animals you choose to draw provide insights and important messages about yourself. A drawing of an animal can signify who you are in the moment or who you might become. Each animal has strengths and characteristics that you can relate to. I once had a client choose a turtle and relate it to moving slowly through life. Yet, when we discussed the turtle further, she began to realize that moving slowly is not necessarily a negative characteristic. It's a way to stop the rush and enjoy life's little moments.

STEPS:

1. Take some time to choose three animals. The first animal should represent you physically (how you move or look), the second animal should represent you emotionally (how you feel), and the last animal should represent you cognitively (how you think).

2. Use the pencil to draw the three animals on a of sheet paper. Don't get wrapped up in trying to draw the animals perfectly. Be creative and draw the animals as you see or feel fit. If you need help, try using an image of the animal for inspiration.

3. Add the environments in which the animals live (mountains, valley, jungle, house, zoo, etc.). Multiple habitats can be captured on the same sheet of paper.

4. Now that your pencil sketch is complete, trace over the pencil lines with the black pen.

5. Use the colored pencils to color in the image.

Questions for Discussion:

- Discuss each animal's strengths. How do their strengths relate to you?

- How can you use these strengths to help cope with a life situation?

- How can the animals you've chosen live together?

Feeling Wheel

BENEFIT:

Identifies feelings to gain mastery over emotions

Exercise time:
50 minutes

MATERIALS:

Drawing pencil

1 sheet of 18-by-24-inch heavy-weight drawing paper

Colored pencils

Oil pastels

A first step in emotional regulation can be connecting with an emotion on the Feeling Wheel. Identifying current emotions is important to the development of self-awareness. This exercise will assist you in recognizing your emotions by naming and discussing them. If you're struggling with expressing a particular emotion, you might want to start with one of these emotions to see what resonates with you: happiness, joy, sadness, apathy, boredom, anger, rage, frustration, love, shock, anxiety, or disgust.

STEPS:

1. Using a pencil, draw a large circle on your paper. If you need help drawing a circle, trace a round object. A kitchen bowl is easy to use for this purpose.

2. Divide the circle into eight triangles (like a pie).

3. On the edge of each triangle, write a feeling. When you're done, you should have eight triangles with eight feelings written at the top of each triangle.

4. Choose a color that you closely associate with the feeling you have written, and color in the triangle with a combination of colored pencils and oil pastels. Be sure not to color over the feeling you've listed. Do this for each of the eight triangles.

Questions for Discussion:

- Which feelings did you write down first?

- Which feelings are you currently experiencing?

- Did you color any two emotions the same color?
  If you did, what does this mean to you?

- Are there more positive emotions or negative ones on
  your Feeling Wheel?

In a Group Setting: Instruct each person to evaluate
their own work quietly. Afterward, group members can
share their personal analysis with others.

Emotional Landscape

BENEFIT:

Identifies feelings to gain mastery over emotions

Prep time:
5 minutes

Exercise time:
45 minutes

MATERIALS:

1 sheet of 18-by-24-inch heavy-weight drawing paper

Drawing pencil

Paintbrush

Watercolors

Cup of water

An emotional landscape is a metaphor for how you feel. This is an opportunity to explore your feelings in a symbolic way. How do your current emotions translate into a scene? Think of your landscape as having a background, middle ground, and foreground. Be creative with your visualization. Your emotional landscape could be rolling hills, mountains, raging seas, barren desert, or a lush garden. Your emotional landscape may also vary on a daily or weekly basis.

STEPS:

1. Sit for five minutes and evaluate your current state of mind. Consider what feelings and emotions are with you at this moment. Think of a landscape that would visually represent your current mood. Feel free to find images in books or on the Internet to inspire you.

2. On the paper, use a pencil to sketch the landscape you've visualized.

3. With a paintbrush, use the watercolors to add blocks of color to your landscape. You can choose to dip your paintbrush in the water to change colors, or to make a particular color lighter or darker.

4. Give your artwork a title.

Questions for Discussion:

- Does your painting speak to the emotions you're feeling at this moment?

- How long have you been feeling this way?

- If you could shrink in size and jump into your painting, where would you land in the image?

- Is there a message in your painting?

Bridge Drawing

BENEFIT:

Identifies goals, obstacles, and challenges

Exercise time:
55 minutes

MATERIALS:

Drawing pencil

1 sheet of 18-by-24-inch heavy-weight drawing paper

Acrylic paint

Paintbrush

Cup of water

A bridge is a figure of stability and connection. It's a symbol of where you want to go, how you're going to get there, and what obstacles you may have to overcome along the way. Bridges are made of different materials (concrete, steel, wood, and rope) that can affect the journey over the bridge. Imagine the first step taken onto a solid concrete bridge versus the first step onto a rope bridge. Before starting this exercise, consider the material your bridge will be made from.

STEPS:

1. Use a pencil to sketch your bridge on the paper. To the left of the bridge, include imagery of what you're leaving. On the right, identify where you are headed. Under the bridge, draw obstacles you have encountered along the way.

2. Using the paint, color in your artwork.

3. Add yourself to the image. Where are you on this bridge and in this journey? You can indicate your location by adding a dot, a stick figure, or any other symbol you choose to represent yourself.

Questions for Discussion:

- What has prevented you from overcoming the challenges you identified so far?

- How significant are these challenges?

- What are five steps that you can take to overcome these challenges?

Favorite Kind of Day

BENEFITS:

Elevates mood and encourages relaxation and collaboration

Prep time:
5 minutes

Exercise time:
55 minutes

MATERIALS:

Drawing pencil

1 sheet of 18-by-24-inch heavy-weight drawing paper

Colored pencils

Watercolors

Paintbrush

Cup of water

If you could do anything you wanted today, what would it be? Remove all the limits you typically place on yourself—such as financial roadblocks, scheduling conflicts, or other constraints. Thinking outside the box and being open to a limitless day can lift your mood and raise your hope.

STEPS:

1. Spend at least five minutes thinking about what your ideal day would look like. You are free to do whatever you want to do. When would you get up? Would you spend the day alone or with other people? Would you stay home or go elsewhere? Think through all the details.

2. Using a pencil, draw your favorite day on the paper. It can be one scene in one location or it can involve many activities.

3. Using either your colored pencils or watercolors, add color to your drawing.

Questions for Discussion:

- What feelings surfaced as you completed this exercise?

- What activities came up when you thought about how you would want to spend your time?

- If you had the power to choose how you want your life to be, what would that look like for you?

In a Group Setting: Exchange drawings with another person and add elements to their drawing. Adding to someone else's drawing creates cohesion within a group and strengthens the communal connection. It's also fun to see other people's imaginations at work on your art.

Safe Place

BENEFIT:

Creates a safe place to
help relieve anxiety

Exercise time:
50 minutes

MATERIALS:

1 sheet of 18-by-24-inch
heavy-weight
drawing paper

Assorted markers

Colored pencils

Oil pastels

Creating a safe place on paper can assist you in relieving anxiety when you experience a trigger. A trigger is a noise, smell, or sight that makes you feel panicked because it's associated with a negative experience. A trauma trigger is a stimulus that transports you back to the original trauma. Triggers are different for everyone. The Safe Place drawing can be used as a visual image to help you think of a safe space when triggers occur. The purpose of creating a safe place is to allow you to relax and bring feelings of security to mind. If your trauma was too intense and you find it difficult to think of an image of a safe place, try using a metaphor. Examples include a sunset, a beach scene, or a clubhouse.

STEPS:

1. Think of a place where you feel most comfortable (outside, inside, or a fantasy world). For example, the beach may bring you a sense of calm. Or, maybe it's your bedroom. Or, a magical castle.

2. On your paper, use markers, colored pencils, or oil pastels to create this space. Be sure to add details and colors that make you feel at ease.

Questions for Discussion:

- Are there associations that make you feel uncomfortable?

- Are there places, smells, or people that create positive thoughts and feelings of safety? Identify a few.

- Knowing what your triggers are allows you to prepare yourself for coping with a situation. What other tools, such as talking to a friend, writing in your journal, or meditation, can help you cope?

Life-Size Body Mapping

BENEFITS:

Improves self-concept, self-awareness, and personal strengths

Exercise time:
1 hour

MATERIALS:

Sheet of butcher paper measured to your height

Drawing pencil

Masking tape

Acrylic paint

Assorted paintbrushes

Cup of water

This exercise will show you how to use different parts of your body to communicate how you feel. It will also help you recognize how you feel about different areas of your body. Are you holding stress in a certain area? Which parts of yourself do you like? One of my clients who wanted to have a gender confirmation surgery painted large horizontal lines over her chest. It gave her the opportunity to express her dislike with her current body and sparked a conversation of the changes she would like to make in the future. She was also able to find areas of her body that she still loved.

STEPS:

1. Place the butcher paper on the floor.
2. Lie on the butcher paper and trace yourself with a pencil. You may have to sit up to trace the bottom half of your body.
3. Hang the butcher paper on the wall with masking tape.
4. Inside the outline of your body, use the paint to illustrate what's going on inside you. Include both physical and mental feelings and thoughts.
5. Use lines and colors to represent your energy and how you feel.
6. Identify on your image where you hold strength in your body.

Questions for Discussion:

- What is it like to be yourself right now?

- Where are you holding your strengths and why?

- Where are you holding your stress and why?

- Think about how this information applies to your life. If there is something you don't like about yourself, can you make a change?

- How can you celebrate the parts that you love about yourself?

In a Group Setting: Pair off with someone to help you outline your body on the butcher paper. It's important to have trust between partners for this step.

Attaining Power

BENEFIT:

Improves constructive coping skills

Prep time:
5 minutes

Exercise time:
45 minutes

MATERIALS:

Drawing pencil

1 sheet of 18-by-24-inch heavy-weight drawing paper

Acrylic paint

Paintbrush

Cup of water

Colored pencils

Inner strength and confidence can help you handle challenging times. Personal power is about being adaptable to situations in life, taking responsibility for your actions, and being able to express your needs and desires. When you can effectively manage your emotions, you will feel powerful. You have the power to choose how you respond to life events. When you use coping tools to manage emotions, you will inevitably see a shift in your life. Once you understand and embrace your power, you will be able to achieve your goals.

STEPS:

1. Spend at least five minutes thinking of a symbol that represents your personal power. This may be a symbol used for protection or something used to embody your current strength.

2. Once you visualize what this symbol looks like, use a pencil to sketch it on the paper.

3. Color your sketch, using either paint or colored pencils.

Questions for Discussion:

- Where in your life do you lack power?

- Dig deep and look at your day. When do you give away your power throughout the day?

- For some people, carrying an object like a charm or a crystal helps because it represents power to them, and it can bring them strength. What object can serve this purpose for you?

Healing Symbols

BENEFITS:

Increases self-esteem and coping skills

Exercise time:

50 minutes

MATERIALS:

Computer

1 sheet of 18-by-24-inch heavy-weight drawing paper

Tracing paper

Pencil

Acrylic paint

Paintbrushes

Cup of water

Symbols can have many interpretations according to a person's beliefs. Healing symbols are images that evoke peace and are very personal. Finding strength in symbols can feel empowering. You can find inspiration from animals, logos, nature, or everyday objects. Many of my clients choose a butterfly because it's a symbol of transformation and change. Other clients pick flowers as a sign of hope, or an animal to promote self-empowerment. When times become challenging, you can refer to your healing symbol as a support mechanism. Consider hanging your healing symbols in your home as a reminder of your self-development.

STEPS:

1. Choose a symbol that represents your healing process.
2. Print an image of this symbol from the Internet.
3. Use tracing paper and a pencil and transfer the image to paper. If you don't have tracing paper, you could use your computer screen as a lightbox. Place a piece of paper over the computer screen and trace the image.
4. Fill in the image with paint and add color to the background.

Questions for Discussion:

- Did anything emerge in your piece that surprised you?
- How can you incorporate your symbol into your day?

Traumatic Moments

BENEFITS:

Recalls trauma and
processes emotions

Exercise time:
50 minutes

MATERIALS:

Drawing pencil

1 sheet of 18-by-24-inch
heavy-weight
drawing paper

Colored pencils

Traumatic events can include natural disasters, serious accidents, terrorist acts, wars/combat, assaults, and other violent crimes. Individuals with PTSD may experience symptoms months or years after the event. Symptoms of PTSD can include nightmares, unwanted memories of the event, heightened reactions, anxiety, or depression. This exercise will help you clarify the order of the events that took place right before, during, and after the traumatic event. Many people who experience a traumatic event have difficulty recalling the details because they were in shock. By drawing out the events, it can help you retell the story to integrate it into your memory.

STEPS:

1. Use a drawing pencil to draw three lines to divide the paper into equal sections.

2. In the first section, use the colored pencils to draw your life before the traumatic event. In the second section, draw the traumatic event. In the third section, draw your life after the event.

3. Then, on the back of the paper, write your emotional responses to the retelling of your story. **NOTE:** Contact a trained therapist from the American Art Therapy Association website if you need help processing your feelings.

Questions for Discussion:

- What support systems have you put in place to process emotions?

- How would you retell your story now to integrate the event into your life?

Garden of Self

BENEFITS:

Promotes self-awareness and helps recognize personal strengths and weaknesses

Prep time:
5 minutes

Exercise time:
45 minutes

MATERIALS:

1 sheet of 18-by-24-inch heavy-weight drawing paper

Assorted markers

Oil pastels

Gardens are beautiful metaphors for life. One of my favorite quotes is, "A flower does not think of competing with the flower next to it. It just blooms." We are all on our own path, yet we need to be nurtured, just like a garden. In this exercise the garden is symbolic of your headspace. Tending to your garden can bring about challenges and rewards. Creating your garden will assist in identifying your goals and obstacles that may prevent you from reaching them.

STEPS:

1. Take five minutes to imagine a garden of self as a metaphor. The healthy plants represent your positive strengths and attributes, the seeds represent your goals, and the weeds represent the issues or problems that prevent you from reaching your goals.

2. Using markers and oil pastels, draw your positive strengths as healthy plants.

3. Draw the goals that you want to achieve as seeds (or sprouting plants).

4. Draw weeds to represent what could prevent you from achieving your goals.

5. Add other details needed to tend to your garden.

Questions for Discussion:

- How would you describe your garden's plants, seeds, and weeds?

- What are some ways that you can maintain your garden?

- What are the next steps to get rid of the weeds and nurture the seeds in your life?

Visual Metaphor of Your Life

BENEFIT:

Identifies feelings to gain mastery over emotion

Prep time:
15 minutes

Exercise time:
45 minutes

MATERIALS:

1 sheet of 18-by-24-inch heavy-weight drawing paper

Colored pencils

Watercolors

Paintbrushes

Cup of water

Take time to think about your current life. What metaphors come to mind? One effective metaphor for life is a landscape. Think of the feelings that come over you when you look at a landscape of violently blowing trees compared with a landscape of gently rolling hills with low grass. One of my favorite metaphorical images is a scene of just red doors. My client drew the doors to open away from her as if they were opening to the future and leading to new life opportunities. Think of different objects that would symbolize your life right now, or where you're heading.

STEPS:

1. Take 15 minutes to reflect on your life. What metaphor represents your current situation?

2. Sketch a visual representation of your metaphor on the paper with the colored pencils.

3. Use the watercolors to add more color to your art.

Questions for Discussion:

- What emotions surfaced while painting?

- What feelings are associated with your current experiences in life?

- It's important to be honest about your feelings in order to feel them and then to release them. Is there another image of how you would like to experience life? Write your thoughts in your journal.

Heart Strings Drawing

BENEFIT:

Improves emotional regulation and coping skills

Exercise time:
1 hour

MATERIALS:

Printed image of an outline of a heart

1 sheet of 18-by-24-inch heavy-weight drawing paper

Scissors

Glue

Colored pencils

Acrylic paint

Paintbrushes

Cup of water

Many people hold stress in their heart, which is both physically and mentally dangerous. Drawing a heart and adding metaphorical color provides an opportunity to heal emotions by creating a tangible way to confront the stress in your heart. A way to tackle stress is to develop coping tools such as gratitude, support from friends, talking to someone, forgiveness, helping someone else, or making an art date.

STEPS:

1. Print out an outline of a heart from the Internet or, if you prefer, draw a large heart on the sheet of paper with the colored pencils. If you've printed a heart from the Internet, cut out the outline and then use glue to paste the heart on the paper.

2. Inside the heart, write the feelings that your heart is holding at this moment. Using acrylic paint, match the emotions you feel to the different colors.

3. In the area surrounding your heart, list the coping skills that will help you to heal. If you like, you can draw heart strings (lines) coming out from your heart, and then list the coping skills on those lines.

Questions for Discussion:

- What feelings has your heart been holding?
- How long have you been feeling this way?
- What does your heart need from you?
- How will you incorporate new coping skills into your life?

Pick an Affirmation

BENEFITS:

Creates a positive mindset, and improves problem solving and decision making skills

Exercise time:
1 hour

MATERIALS:

Computer

Strip of paper

Drawing pencil

Acrylic paint

Paintbrushes

Cup of water

Small Mason jar

Affirmations are powerful statements that aim to bring about a new mindset and change limiting beliefs. Through the process of writing and repeatedly reading an affirmation, you can program your brain to believe the affirmation is true. In this exercise, you will choose an affirmation to help you with a current challenge. For example, if you're struggling with self-esteem, your affirmation could be, "I'm learning to love myself." Powerful self-statements can transform into beliefs.

STEPS:

1. Browse the Internet and find a positive affirmation that resonates with you.

2. Write the affirmation down on a strip of paper with a pencil.

3. With the affirmation you selected in mind, think of an image that represents it.

4. Using paint, create this image on the Mason jar.

5. Once the paint is dry, place the affirmation strip in the jar and close the lid.

6. Place your completed art in a location where you'll see it every day.

Questions for Discussion:

- How does the affirmation you chose relate to your life?

- What other affirmations can you add to your list?

In a Group Setting: Each person creates their own message related to a current challenge. Participants can help each other select affirmations or provide ideas. Once the image is complete, each member can explain their art.

Family Drawing

BENEFIT:

Increases understanding of family dynamics as they relate to emotional issues

Prep time:
5 minutes

Exercise time:
45 minutes

MATERIALS:

Drawing pencil

1 sheet of 18-by-24-inch heavy-weight drawing paper

Colored pencils

Oil pastels

Childhood experiences can play a large role in the relationships we have today. Looking back on these relationships can help you identify emotional issues that may challenge you. In this exercise, you will explore the emotional dynamics between you and each of your family members, as well as delve into how they influenced your upbringing.

STEPS:

1. Take five minutes to reflect on which members of your family have been important in your life. Determine who, if anyone, has been an essential part of your journey.

2. Use a pencil to draw those family members onto paper. Be sure to include yourself in your drawing.

3. Use colored pencils and oil pastels to add color to your art.

Questions for Discussion:

- Does the person you are standing next to relate to who you are closest to emotionally?

- How has their presence or absence in your life shaped who you are today?

- Is there anyone with whom you would like to nurture a stronger relationship?

Painting Mandala

BENEFITS:

Improves group cohesion, communication, stress relief, and meditation skills

Exercise time:
1 hour

MATERIALS:

Drawing pencil

Large sheet of butcher paper

Scissors

Acrylic paint

Paintbrush

Cup of water

Mandala is the Sanskrit word for circle. It is used in Eastern traditions as a tool of meditation. The actual act of creating the mandala is the meditation. Mandalas include shapes and symbols that you create intuitively. Many mandalas have a repeated pattern of shapes that make a cohesive design. The intention of this exercise is to relax through the process of creating art. Forty-five minutes of art making has been shown to have a direct correlation with decreasing levels of the stress hormone cortisol.

STEPS:

1. Use a pencil to draw a large circle onto the sheet of butcher paper and then cut the circle out.

2. Find a comfortable seated position and place the paint and paintbrush in front of you.

3. Practice a simple breathing exercise to help you calm down and focus. For example, breathe in for a count of 4, hold for a count of 4, then release for a count of 6. Repeat 3 times.

4. Use the paint to create repeated patterns within the circle.

Questions for Discussion:

- Were you able to reach a deep meditative place while working on this art?

- What is the story behind your artwork?

- Why did you choose the colors you used?

In a Group Setting: While sitting in a circle around the butcher paper, members will work together to create patterns on the mandala. If group members are unable to sit together, divide the paper circle into equal parts, matching the number of group members. Ask group members to work in silence. Once everyone is finished, have members bring the pieces together to reform the circle and share the part they worked on. Working together in this way creates cohesion and a relaxing environment.

Strength Shield

BENEFIT:

Identifies personal strengths

Exercise time:
50 minutes

MATERIALS:

Drawing pencil

1 sheet of 18-by-24-inch heavy-weight drawing paper

Scissors

Colored pencils

Oil pastels

Shields are known for their protective symbolism and strength. They are made of heavy metal and were once used to protect soldiers during battle. Their unique coats of arms represent who they meant to protect. In this exercise you will create your own strength shield. Your design should be thought of as a protective force to empower you during times of turmoil. Think of your own strengths and how they are used to protect you. Maybe you are creative, and you use your creativity as an outlet to cope?

STEPS:

1. Draw a shield on the paper. If you need help, search for a shield shape on the Internet and trace it onto your piece of paper.

2. Cut out the shield.

3. Use the pencil to divide your shield into four equal parts.

4. Identify four of your strengths, and write each one in a separate part of your shield.

5. Use the colored pencils and oil pastels to add color to your art. Try using only colors that represent strength to you.

Questions for Discussion:

- Do you shield yourself from others? In what ways?

- How can you use your strengths to connect more with those around you?

Feeling Chart

BENEFITS:

Identifies personal feelings and helps gain mastery and regulation over emotions

Exercise time:
50 minutes

MATERIALS:

1 sheet of 18-by-24-inch heavy-weight drawing paper

Scissors

Pen

Colored pencils

Oil pastels

Each of our emotions relates to specific experiences. In this exercise you will be asked to draw an experience in which you've related to various emotions. This is an opportunity to reflect on the last time you experienced each emotion. I've had clients who have had a difficult time remembering the last time they felt genuine feelings of happiness. It's important to nurture your inner world and allow yourself to appreciate and enjoy life.

STEPS:

1. Cut the sheet of paper into 8 equal squares.

2. Use a pen to assign a feeling to each square. For example, you could list one of the following in each square: joy, frustration, hate, love, anxiety, sadness, boredom, and excitement.

3. With the colored pencils or oil pastels, draw an image or scene on each square that depicts the last time you experienced the emotion you have listed in that square.

Questions for Discussion:

- Look at each emotion. To which squares did you add the most details and give the most attention?

- Which emotions do you want to experience more of?

- What can you do today to nurture that experience?

Guided Garden Visualization

BENEFIT:

Increases problem-solving and coping skills

Exercise time:
55 minutes

MATERIALS:

2 sheets of 18-by-24-inch heavy-weight drawing paper

Drawing pencil

Oil pastels

A guided visualization is a technique where you imagine a scene and then draw it out. If you feel comfortable, you can close your eyes to imagine the scenes. In this exercise, you are going to visualize and draw a journey that has four different scenes. It's a technique used to identify current coping skills and desires. Each drawing task is geared toward determining how you respond and problem solve.

STEPS:

1. Fold each paper in half and then number each half with 1 through 4.

2. Take a comfortable seated position and place the materials in front of you.

3. Imagine you are by yourself, and you have reserved the day to go on a journey. You are looking forward to your adventure. You pack a bag and head to a large green field. As you walk through the field you come to a beautiful fence with a gate that reads, "Welcome." You try to open the gate, but it's stuck.

4. How do you get through the gate? Draw your response on page 1.

5. Congratulations! You made it through the gate. On the other side of the gate, there is a luscious flower and vegetable garden before you. You take your time to smell the flowers and taste some fruit. The bounty is delicious. As you walk the path, a large creature appears in front of your feet. What do you do? Draw your response on page 2.

6. Congratulations! You made it past this challenge. As you continue, the path turns into a denser forest. You suddenly realize you have been on this journey for a long time, as the sun starts to set and the sky darkens. It's too late to turn back so you decide to settle in the forest for

the evening. You see a cute little wooden cabin ahead. As you approach the cabin, a being appears. What do you do? Draw your response on page 3.

7. Congratulations! This being grants you permission to use their cabin and then disappears. The cabin has everything you need in a quaint space. As you settle in for the night and close your eyes, you hear a noise inside the cabin. You're not alone. What else is in the cabin? Draw your response on page 4.

8. Read the story aloud as if you were narrating the entire journey to either yourself or to a partner or therapist.

Questions for Discussion:

- In the first drawing you are asked to open a gate. How did you get through the gate?

- In the second drawing, a creature is in front of you. How did you respond? Did you use force, compromise, or run?

- Identify who or what you saw in the third and fourth drawings. How did you react to them? Who or what you saw is symbolic of your unconscious mind.

- You can use the chart below to determine if your actions were passive, assertive, or aggressive. Do you like the ways you responded? If not, you have the power to make a change.

PASSIVE	ASSERTIVE	AGGRESSIVE
run away	give something	use force
freeze up	interact (speak)	hit, touch, scare, kill

Stress in the Body

BENEFITS:

Identifies feelings and increases self-awareness

Exercise time:
45 minutes

MATERIALS:

1 sheet of 18-by-24-inch heavy-weight drawing paper

Drawing pencil

Paintbrushes

Watercolors

Cup of water

Stress is the state of mental or emotional tension resulting from demanding circumstances. Many people live their day-to-day lives in this state of discomfort. When you hold stress in your body, it can manifest into physical pain. In this exercise, you will visualize what stress looks like in order to help uncover its source. Stress can be focused in a specific area of the body or found in multiple areas. I have seen my clients identify where they hold their stress, what has caused it, and then work to alleviate it.

STEPS:

1. On paper, draw an outline of your body with a head, torso, arms, and legs.

2. Draw the stress that exists in your body. Consider what form stress takes in regard to shape and size, and where it resides.

3. Use paint to add color to your art, selecting bolder colors to bring attention to stress in the body.

Questions for Discussion:

- Where in your body did you identify your stress?

- How long have you been experiencing stress in certain areas of your body?

- Have you tried to address this stress previously?

- What are ways you can remove stress? For example, could the stress in your back be alleviated through a massage?

Building Boundaries, Not Walls

BENEFITS:

Develops coping skills and emotional regulation

Prep time:
30 minutes

Exercise time:
30 minutes

MATERIALS:

Assorted markers

1 sheet of 18-by-24-inch heavy-weight drawing paper

Assorted printed paper (newspapers, wrapping paper, designed paper)

Scissors

Glue

Sometimes it's difficult to know when to express your emotions to others, but you can learn to meet your needs without overwhelming your family, coworkers, or friends. Having healthy boundaries means knowing where your limits are. For example, you might not want to divulge your personal life to a coworker or a new friend. It's important to step back and look at your needs in every relationship. What do your boundary walls look like?

STEPS:

1. Take 30 minutes to identify the limits on where you feel comfortable with the people in your life on physical, emotional, and spiritual levels.

2. Give yourself permission to say no.

3. With the markers, draw yourself in the middle of the paper.

4. Glue the assorted papers around your portrait to create a healthy boundary wall.

5. Identify one person you need to establish boundaries for, and draw them outside your healthy boundaries wall.

Questions for Discussion:

- Do you have any walls between you and your friends, coworkers, romantic partners, or children? Are there any walls that prevent you from nurturing yourself?

- How big are your walls? Are your walls so tall that no one can get in?

- How can you create healthy boundaries in order to express your feelings? Is there anything in your life that you would like to say "no" to?

Chapter Three

DIGITAL AND PHOTOS

DIGITAL ART AND PHOTOGRAPHIC IMAGES CAN evoke memories, prompt you to narrate stories about your life, and motivate you to become involved in the psychological healing process. The process of observing and choosing images will help you take owner-ship of your psychological state. It may have been damaged during traumatic experiences, such as the unexpected death of a loved one, abuse, family violence, war, terrorism, natural disasters, or chronic illness. Digital storytelling, photo therapy, and memory books are among the modalities for healing discussed in this chapter.

Photo Transfer Self-Portrait

BENEFITS:

Increases personal reflection and self-awareness

Exercise time:
1 hour

MATERIALS:

Photo of yourself

1 sheet 18-by-24-inch heavy-weight paper

Mod Podge®

Acrylic paint

Paintbrushes

Cup of water

The age-old question, "Who am I?" comes to mind when you work on a self-portrait. An image of yourself can bring revelation and insight. Your true self will come through as you create your self-portrait. The details you depict and the colors you choose are an extension of you. Before you get started, ask yourself how you would like to be remembered and how you think others see you. Also contemplate your best qualities.

STEPS:

1. Choose an image of yourself from the past or present. Make a photocopy of this image, either in black and white or color.

2. Apply a layer of Mod Podge® to your paper.

3. Place your image on the Mod Podge®, and then layer Mod Podge® on top of the photo. Allow it to dry for 20 minutes.

4. Use the paint to add color and emotional expression to your art.

Questions for Discussion:

- How did you use the paint to add emotional expression?

- Do you feel your artwork is a representation of who you are now or of your ideal self?

Being Seen

BENEFITS:

Improves problem-solving,
self-esteem, and
self-reflection

Prep time:
10 minutes

Exercise time:
50 minutes

MATERIALS:

Paper

Pen

Digital camera

This activity is about creating a version of yourself that represents of how you would like to be seen. It's about manifesting your ideal self. How do you want to feel? This exercise is about creating that feeling and then making it visual. By taking the steps to create the feeling in an image, you will manifest it in real life. Be outrageous. If you want to create freedom in your life, what could give you that feeling? Maybe it's driving a fancy car? You could go test drive one at a dealership and do a photo shoot! There are no limits to your imagination. Dream big!

STEPS:

1. Spend 10 minutes deciding how you want to be seen.

2. Make a list of feeling words that describe how you will feel when you are seen this way.

3. Write out ideas of fun activities that you can do to create the feeling in real life.

4. Take photographs of yourself doing these activities.

Questions for Discussion:

- How does it feel to see your dream in a photograph?

- What is another step you can take to make your ideal self come to life?

Mini Mind Movie

BENEFITS:

Identifies strengths, imagines positive experiences, and manifests future events

Prep time:
10 minutes

Exercise time:
50 minutes

MATERIALS:

Computer

PowerPoint software

A mind movie is a snapshot of the life you desire. It allows you to see life in the present, as if what you have imagined is already in your possession. Consider positive events from your current life that have brought you joy. What if you could manifest similar experiences? It's important to view your mind movie daily to bring about good feelings and add clarity to what you desire out of your life.

STEPS:

1. Take 10 minutes to brainstorm what you desire out of life.
2. Type one of your desires onto a PowerPoint presentation slide.
3. Find an image to match that desire and place it on the next slide.
4. Repeat the process to create several slides using your desires and images. You can use images from the Internet as well as from your own life.
5. Consider adding your favorite song to the presentation.
6. Watch your presentation in slideshow mode once a day.

Questions for Discussion:

- How does it feel to dream big?
- The first step in manifesting a desire is having a vision. How did it feel to see positive events and affirmations in your life?

Pinterest Mood Boards

BENEFIT:

Identifies current emotions

Exercise time:
50 minutes

MATERIALS:

Computer

Pinterest website

The Pinterest platform allows you to create a variety of mood boards and see them all together. You can search for images that resonate with your every mood. I had a client create several boards on a weekly basis. She liked to document things that inspired her and then send the boards to me to view. We were able to see what was going on in her life, and the best part—no cleanup.

STEPS:

1. From a browser, go to Pinterest.com. If you prefer, there is a Pinterest application available for your smartphone.
2. Sign up or log in.
3. Create a board and title it: Mood Board.
4. Search in the finder tab for objects, places, colors, and images that resonate with your current mood and place them on your Mood Board.

Questions for Discussion:

- As you created your board, did a theme emerge? What was it?
- Did you get sidetracked and start looking at other websites or blogs?
- Did you find other images that you wanted to save? You can save these for when you want to create paintings.

Positive Affirmations

BENEFITS:

Builds self-esteem, changes mindset, and addresses limited beliefs

Exercise time:
1 hour

MATERIALS:

Paper

Drawing pencil

Smartphone

Creating a positive affirmation is empowering! Affirmations can give emotional support or encouragement when you need it. I like to keep positive affirmations in my phone as daily reminders of the power I have to change. Creating a digital image to go with your affirmation gives it even more impact. In some situations, you can physically change a problem, and in other cases you might need to mentally change your outlook. You may have to try out both solutions to see which one is a better fit for a given situation.

STEPS:

1. On the paper, write down a challenge you are currently facing.

2. Next to your challenge, write 3 to 5 positive solutions.

3. Create an affirmation to match the positive solutions.

4. Take a photo with your phone that is inspired by your positive solution.

5. Add your affirmation to your picture using your phone editor (add text or play with the lighting).

6. Save your art as screensaver on your phone and/or computer.

Questions for Discussion:

- How can you use this affirmation throughout your day?

- How did it feel to come up with a positive, proactive solution to your issue?

Three Portraits of You

BENEFITS:
Fosters self-reflection and creative expression

Exercise time:
1 hour

MATERIALS:
Camera

Self-portraits are reflections of how you view yourself and can give you insight into how you are perceived. Creating three portraits at the same time can be transformational because you're able to view different aspects of yourself at the same time. In this exercise you can use parts of your body or the full view. You can take into account your physical features and create emotional images through body language.

STEPS:
1. Take a photo of how you see yourself.
2. Take a photo of how you think others see you.
3. Take a photo of how you would like to be seen.

Questions for Discussion:
- Which portrait was the easiest to create? Which one was the most difficult?
- Do you see any similarities between the portraits?
- What are the differences between the three?

Traditional Memory Book

BENEFIT:

Reviews memories and relationships to help you better understand family dynamics

Prep time:
10 minutes

Exercise time:
50 minutes

MATERIALS:

Memory books/photo albums from the past

Printed images of present time

Blank memory book

Memorabilia (ticket stubs, receipts, journal notes, love letters, photographs, pressed flowers, etc.)

Memory books provide an opportunity to examine family dynamics over a length of time. Looking back at body language from these images can provide a deeper understanding of the roles certain people played in your life. You can review relationships that were significant, provide the narrative to your story, and also leave room for new memories yet to be captured.

STEPS:

1. Gather memory books and photo albums. If your images are digital, print them onto paper.
2. Examine each photo and think about your relationships with the people in the photographs.
3. Look at the more recent images. Print any images that signify an important time or important people in your life.
4. Place those images of the present in your new memory book.
5. To personalize your memory book, think about adding memorabilia that hold significance for you.

Questions for Discussion:

- How have your family and heritage influenced who you are today?
- Where are you headed?

In a Group Setting: When in a group, complete the above steps and then discuss your family heritages and traditions with each other.

Digital Memory Book

BENEFITS:

Processes memories, develops coping skills, and identifies support systems

Prep time:
10 minutes

Exercise time:
50 minutes

MATERIALS:

Computer

A digital memory book lets you electronically organize your photos into one place. It allows you to give a narrative of your life events and identify your support systems. You can add favorite songs, messages, traditions, or even recipes that are important to your family. You can even include a video message to someone if you would like to share it. Digital memory books can be stored in a central location that can be shared with people who are important to you. The best part of the digital memory book is that they don't take up much space beyond storage on a flash drive or a hard drive.

STEPS:

1. Locate 5 to 10 personal images from your past and present. Be sure to include several of you with other people.

2. Visit a digital website where you can create a digital photo album. Two sites that I recommend are FamilyTreeGuide.com and Ancestry.com.

3. After you've created a profile on the website of your choice, upload your images.

4. Organize your uploaded images chronologically.

5. This exercise can be either completed in one sitting or over time, whichever you prefer.

Questions for Discussion:

- What relationships are represented in your photos?

- Why did you choose those relationships to share in your photo album?

- What do those relationships mean to you?

- Are there periods of time that were particularly significant to you?

Image Altering

BENEFITS:

Relieves stress and improves decision-making skills

Prep time:
10 minutes

Exercise time:
50 minutes

MATERIALS:

Image altering software or application

Computer

Printer (optional)

Image altering allows you to transform existing images and use your decision-making skills. There are a million ways to change an image and you have the power to choose what you like. There really isn't a right or wrong decision in this process—do what feels good to you.

STEPS:

1. Take 10 minutes to choose a favorite photo.
2. Open or download an image altering application (free software can be downloaded online).
3. Add art, text, textures, and filters to transform your photo. If during this image-altering process you don't like a result, you can always revert back to your original image.
4. Save your work.
5. Print the image if you like.

Questions for Discussion:

- Why is this image important to you?
- How has altering the image made it better?

Sadness Imagery

BENEFITS:

Improves problem-solving, decision-making, and self-awareness

Prep time:
10 minutes

Exercise time:
50 minutes

MATERIALS:

Pen

Paper

Camera

There are varying degrees of sadness. There are feelings of being low-spirited, truly unhappy, and dejected. Taking photos is a way to lift your spirit. It helps you slow down. It forces you to take time for yourself and discover your world. You can use photography to document the varying degrees of the feelings of depression.

STEPS:

1. Take at least 10 minutes to think of the different variations for the feeling of sadness.
2. Write down all the variations you thought of on the paper.
3. Go outside and take photographs of different variations of depression.

Questions for Discussion:

- Is there anyone who will go and take pictures with you?
- What were the varying degrees of depression in your photos?
- Are you resonating with any of the images right now?

Photo Nature Therapy Walk

BENEFITS:

Identifies emotions and relieves stress

Exercise time:
1 hour

MATERIALS:

Camera

Printer (optional)

Taking time to walk in nature can be relaxing, and that may help you be more aware and present in the moment. In this exercise you will practice mindfulness by becoming aware of your breath and the steps you take. Taking the time to slow down and consciously work to make yourself aware of your immediate surroundings helps relieve stress and identify emotions.

STEPS:

1. Go for a 30-minute walk in nature. Walk slowly and pay attention to the details in your environment. Force yourself to examine all the things you see at a more exhaustive level than you may have previously.

2. While you walk, pay attention to your breathing. Take deep, slow breaths and feel the air fill your lungs.

3. As you continue to walk, focus your attention on your surroundings, and work to quiet your mind. As day-to-day thoughts come into your mind, such as what you need to do tomorrow, let them come in and then let them flow out.

4. Look for things in the environment that visually interest you.

5. If you see something that is beautiful or strikes an emotion, take a photo of it.

6. Throughout your walk, take images of anything that evokes an emotion.

7. Give each of your photos a name.

8. If you have a printer available, you may want to print a few of your photos to remind yourself of the emotion you felt in that moment. For example, if you took a picture of a lake because it was calming, you may want to leave a copy of that picture it in your desk drawer to refer to it when you are feeling stressed.

Questions for Discussion:

- When you get home, review your images. Do you feel the emotions you felt when you took the photos?

- Have your feelings changed since you originally took them?

Artistic Photo with Narrative

BENEFITS:

Identifies emotions and improves emotional expression

Exercise time:
1 hour

MATERIALS:

Camera

Printer (optional)

Drawing pencil

Paper

Talking about depression and anxiety is a very personal experience and can be quite difficult. To heal, it's important to work through your thoughts and feelings so that you may pull apart the driving factors that result in pain. Finding an image to represent your anxiety or depression can be a gateway for expressing your authentic self.

STEPS:

1. Go outside and look for an object or scene that captures how you currently feel.
2. Take a few photos of that image.
3. Title each of your photographs.
4. Print your images (optional).
5. Sit down and write a narrative on the paper about your photographs and the feelings the images evoked in you.

Questions for Discussion:

- Look at your image with the perspective of another person who is seeing it for the first time. Do you see anything new that you didn't see before?

- Who is the one person you would like to share your photo with? Why did you choose this person?

- What does your chosen title reflect about the feeling you felt when you took the image?

- How much space is there between the subject and background? Is there more than one subject?

Past, Present, and Future Images

BENEFITS:

Identifies feelings, improves self-awareness, and develops decision-making and self-reflection skills

Exercise time:
1 hour

MATERIALS:

1 sheet of 18-by-24-inch heavy-weight drawing paper

Drawing pencil

Photographs

Glue

Magazines

Scissors

This exercise takes you through the process of exploring your own history by working with a few of your personal images. These can include images from childhood, family, relationships, work, leisure activities, or anything else that interests you. As you outline your history on paper, your perspective on the past may change and unexpected emotions may arise. Working through these reactions can help you become more self-aware and help you with future decisions.

STEPS:

1. On the paper, draw 2 overlapping circles so that you create 3 sections.

2. Starting from the left, label these 3 sections as past, present, and future.

3. Glue photos from your past in the past section. (If you don't want to glue your original images, you could use copies instead.)

4. Glue recent photos in the present section.

5. Cut images from the magazines that represent the future you wish to manifest.

6. Glue your future images in the future section.

Questions for Discussion:

- Were you able to find meaningful connections between various periods in your life?

- At any time in creating this art, did powerful emotions overcome you? What were those emotions?

In a Group Setting: Everyone in the group should share their art and discuss where they came from, their current experience, and their plan for manifestation.

Levels of Anxiety

BENEFITS:

Relieves stress, regulates emotions, and improves coping skills

Exercise time:
1 hour

MATERIALS:

Camera

Anxiety is a natural response to stress. Mild anxiety involves an uneasy feeling in your stomach and a slight increase in your pulse. Moderate anxiety involves placing your complete attention on the thing or situation that's making you feel anxious and ignoring everything else around you. Severe anxiety involves repeated episodes of sudden feelings of intense stress and terror that reach a peak within minutes (panic attacks). You may have feelings of impending doom, shortness of breath, chest pain, or heart palpitations. By reviewing and exploring these different levels of anxiety you can learn to understand the emotion and take steps to deal with it constructively. Use imagery that is personal for you and your own levels of anxiety.

STEPS:

1. Take a photo of an image that represents mild anxiety (for example, drinking too much coffee).
2. Take a photo of an image that represents moderate anxiety (for example, being late to an appointment).
3. Take a photo representing severe anxiety (for example, being trapped in an elevator).

Questions for Discussion:

- What are the differences among your photos?
- What are the similarities?
- How can you prevent future anxiety from happening?

Photo Collage

Relieves stress and increases self-esteem and self-awareness

Prep time:
10 minutes

Exercise time:
50 minutes

MATERIALS:

Digital photos from your phone or computer

Printer

Poster board

Glue

Creating a photo collage is a way to combine many positive and powerful experiences into one image. You can choose images that are important to you and arrange them in an aesthetically pleasing way. You can include images from nature walks, photos of friends or interests, or online images. Creating photo collages increases self-esteem and self-awareness. Many of my clients like to collage images from positive experiences as a memory keepsake.

STEPS:

1. Gather your photos. Review them and choose a handful that represents your interest, favorite art, positive memories, and important places and people. Print the selected photos.

2. Arrange your photos in a way that is most pleasing to you. Glue them to the poster board.

3. After your collage is complete, look at it as a total piece of art. Reflect on the positive emotions you feel after creating the art.

Questions for Discussion:

- Who is the one person you would like to share this art with?

- Why did you choose that person?

Manipulating Photos

BENEFITS:

Increases problem-solving skills, identifies emotions, and raises self-awareness

Prep time:
10 minutes

Exercise time:
50 minutes

MATERIALS:

Digital photos from your phone or computer

Printer

Scissors

1 sheet of 18-by-24-inch heavy-weight drawing paper

Glue

Paint pen

In this exercise you will combine two images. This process provides you with practice in making decisions that will create feelings. One of the most interesting image manipulations I have seen was when a client took a self-portrait, cut out their figure, and filled the empty space inside the portrait with landscape art. The eye-opening element in this was that they filled the open space with a powerful and unexpected image.

STEPS:

1. Find two images you'd like to combine. For example, one can be a portrait and the other a landscape.

2. Print those two images.

3. Cut the images out, and glue them to the paper to create one new image. Using the paint pen, add effects to your image that express how you are feeling right at this moment.

Questions for Discussion:

- How do you relate to the combined images?

- What feelings did the images evoke separately? What feelings do they evoke now that they're combined?

What's Your Story?

BENEFITS:

Assists in processing traumatic experiences, and improves emotional regulation, self-reflection, and self-observation skills

Exercise time:
1 hour

MATERIALS:

Computer

PowerPoint software

Images from the Internet

The exercise of telling your story allows you to review your traumatic event and process the emotions involved in that event. The process of reviewing the work allows you to self-reflect and integrate the trauma into your memory. In working through this self-reflection, be sure to identify with being a survivor. Being able to build your story and watch it unfold shows that you are a survivor.

STEPS:

1. Start with a blank PowerPoint slide.

2. On slide 1, start to write your story. Begin at the time before your trauma. Feel free to make it a few paragraphs or several bullet points.

3. Look through personal images and the Internet to find an image that matches your story before your trauma, and add it to this slide. If you don't have space on slide 1, place the image on slide 2.

4. On a new blank slide, start a new paragraph. This time, write about the trauma.

5. Again, look at images and find an image to match your story at that time. Add it to the presentation.

6. Start a new blank slide and write your story of now. What about now distinguishes you from your past?

7. Look through images to find an image to match your current story and add it to your presentation.

8. Once you've finished your work, watch your story in slideshow mode.

Questions for Discussion:

- What were your first thoughts upon watching your story in your slideshow?

- Has watching your story helped you gain perspective on your life experiences?

- What life lessons have you learned from this experience?

Therapeutic Filmmaking

BENEFITS:

Develops self-reflection and self-awareness, and builds coping and emotional regulation skills

Prep time:
10 minutes

Exercise time:
50 minutes

MATERIALS:

Audio and visual recording device such as a smartphone or tablet

Therapeutic filmmaking is similar to traditional filmmaking, but there are fewer steps. The intention is to reflect on past experiences, and process emotions in an effort to lead to a healthier well-being. This process can take multiple sessions.

STEPS:

1. Take 10 minutes to identify a theme for your film. Prompts to help you begin include: Who are you? Where are you from?

2. Create a list of ideas of what you want to include in your film. Think of images, audio, and text that help express your theme.

3. Use your recording device to document your story.

4. Save your film.

5. Watch the film to see it from another perspective.

Questions for Discussion:

- What insights did you learn about yourself as you watched yourself tell your story?

- What would you do differently, if anything, if you could change the outcome of your story?

Safe Place Imagery

BENEFITS:

Relieves anxiety, and increases coping and decision-making skills

Exercise time:

1 hour

MATERIALS:

Camera

PTSD results from surviving a traumatic event. Threatening experiences like war, abuse, or neglect leave traces that get stuck in our memories, emotions, and bodily experiences. When triggered, PTSD causes symptoms such as re-experiencing the trauma, feelings of panic or anxiety, touchiness or reactivity, memory lapses, and numbness or dissociation. Creating a safe place through imagery can help relieve the symptoms of anxiety related to PTSD. Look for spaces and places to photograph that feel safe for you. Be open to creating your own space, if needed. Photo subjects may include a friend, a yoga studio, or a quiet space in a room.

STEPS:

1. Use your camera and take photos of places that feel safe for you.
2. Challenge yourself to create several safe place images.

Questions for Discussion:

- Were there any similarities in the images you chose?
- If you were able to be in one of these images, where would you be most comfortable?
- How can you create more safe places in your environment?

Creative Soul Online Retreat

BENEFITS:

Increases group communication, community support, self-reflection, and coping skills

Exercise time:
50 minutes

MATERIALS:

Computer

Sketchbook

Drawing pencil

The original Creative Soul Online Retreat is a safe and supportive online Facebook group where people have an opportunity to learn about self-care. Within this group people share inspirational posts and feedback on one another's work. Participating in a group is a process that provides immense healing benefits. Many of my clients have a positive experience in the group and feel a nice sense of cohesion and community.

STEPS:

1. Become a member of the Creative Soul Online Retreat Facebook Group at Facebook.com/groups /1668160796774067/. You'll note that I am the administrator.

2. Watch the videos related to self-care.

3. Visit the website daily and follow along with the group art challenges. You can view past videos and challenges by scrolling through the feed.

4. Know that this is a safe and supportive group so you should feel free to post your artwork when you're ready.

5. Monthly meetings take place online. In these meetings we create art together at the same time. This is an effective way to work with others if you don't have easy access to group activities.

Questions for Discussion:

- Have you previously participated in an online community?

- What did you find rewarding or challenging?

- How can you develop an effective community relationship with this new group?

- How do you plan to interact with the other members of this group so that you can become engaged and help others to be engaged?

- What specifically can you do to practice and improve self-reflection through your work with this group?

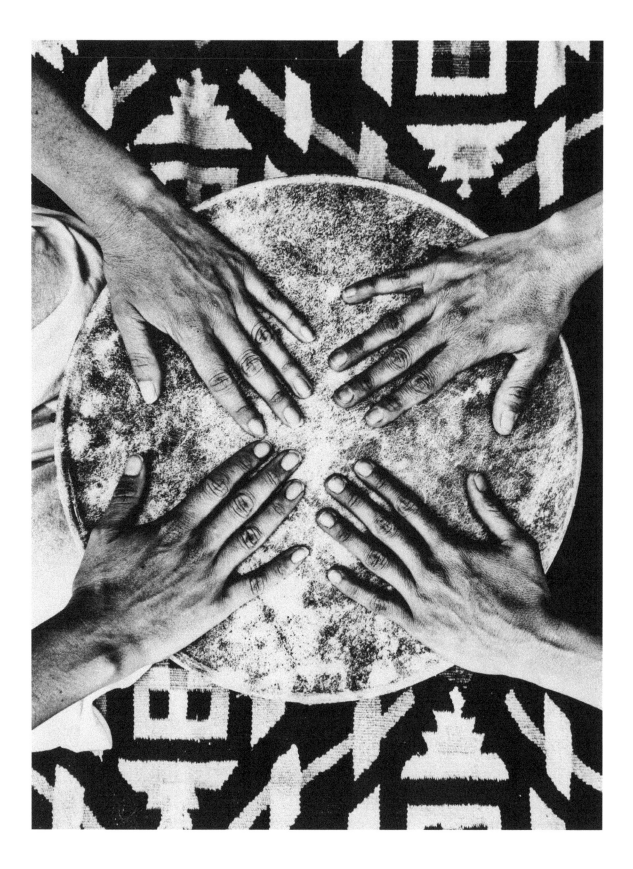

Chapter Four

SCULPTING AND TEXTILES

A SCULPTURE IS A THREE-DIMENSIONAL OBJECT that can be viewed from different angles. The best part of working in three dimensions is the hands-on tactile approach to the creative process. In this chapter, you'll be using a variety of materials—including clay, found objects, plaster, and items from nature—as a way to connect with your emotions.

Feeling Sculpture

BENEFITS:

Decreases stress and assists in identifying emotions

Exercise time:
1 hour

MATERIALS:

Self-drying clay

Small plastic sandwich bag

Acrylic paint

Paintbrushes

Cup of water

The Feeling Sculpture allows you to use your feeling senses to create an abstract shape. This exercise is not about what you create, but about the practice of using your senses. The feeling you have when you squeeze and pinch the clay is an extension of your current emotional state. Working with the clay allows you to objectify what you're feeling. Clients tell me this exercise allows them to pull their emotions outside of their body and, as a result, they feel lighter because they aren't carrying their emotions inside.

STEPS:

1. Place the ball of clay in the plastic bag.
2. Close your eyes.
3. With the clay in the bag, pinch and squeeze the clay. Feel the effects of the clay moving in your fingers.
4. Open your eyes and remove the clay from the bag.
5. Shape the clay into a sculpture. The sculpture could be a random shape or anything else you desire.
6. Let the clay dry.
7. Choose a paint color that represents how you feel.
8. Paint your sculpture with the color you have chosen.
9. Once it's completely dry, place your sculpture in a location where you can easily access it. Use your sculpture as a soothing tool that you roll around in your fingers and your hands.

Questions for Discussion:

* What emotions arose as you created your sculpture?
* What impact do you expect your sculpture to have as you continue to use it as a soothing tool?
* How do you feel after creating the sculpture?

Tin Man Expression

BENEFITS:

Allows the expression of emotions and develops self-awareness

Exercise time:
1 hour

MATERIALS:

Scissors

Ruler

Aluminum foil

Felt

Hot glue gun and glue sticks

The Tin Man Expression is about making a figure to express how you exist in the world. Body language holds emotion. Would your tin man be curled up with arms folded, stand tall with arms out, or sit quietly? Creating a figure related to body language has helped my clients become more aware of their posture throughout the day. It helps improve your awareness of the message you're projecting to others, the message you're sending to yourself, and how you can alter that message by changing your body. For example, if you want to project power or convince yourself that you're powerful at any time, you might stand up with your hands on your hips.

STEPS:

1. Cut three pieces of aluminum foil into 12-by-6-inch squares.
2. Roll the cut pieces into tubes.
3. Fold the first tube in half. These will be the legs for your tin man.
4. Attach the second tube to the middle of the legs. This tube is the head and body.
5. Twist the last tube around the body, creating arms.
6. Arrange the figure to represent how you feel at this moment.
7. Cut the felt and use the glue gun to add the felt pieces to your figure to help represent your feelings.

Questions for Discussion:

- How is your tin man related to how you feel about your place in the world?
- If your tin man could speak, what would they say?

Nature Installation

BENEFITS:

Reduces stress, increases sense of community, and improves problem-solving skills

Prep time:
30 minutes

Exercise time:
30 minutes

MATERIALS:

Objects found in nature (rocks, leaves, sticks, etc.)

Hot glue gun and glue sticks

Spending time in nature can bring a sense of peace and relaxation. Often, nature can help calm or slow down your mind. This scavenger hunt is meant to calm down your mind and help you look at your environment in a new way. Can you pick up a piece of trash and think about how it can be used in a different way? What you find and what you do with it is a metaphor for life. This process represents how you can make something out of nothing.

STEPS:

1. Go for a nature walk.
2. While walking, collect natural objects.
3. Bring your items inside and lay them out. Attach the items together with the hot glue gun to create an art installation.

Questions for Discussion:

- How did you feel while looking for your items in nature?

- Were you able to become more relaxed?

- How did you feel as you pulled the pieces together into an art installation?

- Your art probably won't last long given the materials—and that is intentional. How does it feel to create something that won't last long?

In a Group Setting: Try to create one large installation together.

Flower Expression

BENEFITS:

Relieves stress and develops creative expression

Exercise time:
50 minutes

MATERIALS:

Fresh flowers (either found or bought)

Look at the flowers around you, identify their patterns, and think about how you might arrange them to express your current mood. This process of creative expression can lift your mood and alleviate pressures you may be feeling. My clients often like to take a picture of their final art so that they may capture its beauty for more than a single day.

STEPS:

1. Gather flowers from a nature walk or purchase them from a store. If you prefer, you could work with rocks or leaves instead of flowers.

2. Pick off the flower petals and separate the colors into piles. (Or separate your rocks or leaves into piles by color.)

3. Organize the colors in an aesthetically pleasing way.

4. Verbally dedicate your art to someone.

Questions for Discussion:

- How did it feel to connect with nature in this way?

- Why did you dedicate your beautiful creation to whomever you chose?

Personal Altar

BENEFITS:

Relieves stress and increases coping skills

Prep time:
10 minutes

Exercise time:
50 minutes

MATERIALS:

Inspirational items (flowers or other objects from nature, candles, books, poems, song lyrics, photographs, bells, dolls, crystals, artwork, etc.)

An altar is a personal sacred space dedicated to self-care, spirituality, and positive energy. What do you want to bring more of into your life? Is it peace, healing, abundance, love, protection? This altar in your living space will be a physical reminder to practice self-care daily. In this space you can do the things that bring you peace.

STEPS:

1. Find a location for your altar (for example, a nightstand or the corner of a room). It should be somewhere where your items won't be bothered or moved.

2. Pick at least one theme for your altar. You might choose peace, abundance, protection, healing, or inspiration.

3. Choose 5 to 10 key inspirational items for your altar.

4. Once you have everything in place, bless your altar. Silently or out loud, express your hopes by putting your thoughts into words. This blessing can be as short or as long as you desire.

5. Use your altar by sitting near it and talking about your goals and manifestations.

Questions for Discussion:

- How often will you use your altar?

- How does it feel to take time for yourself?

- How does it feel to claim a space for yourself?

Protection Doll

BENEFITS:

Increases feelings of protection and develops coping skills

Prep time:
10 minutes

Exercise time:
50 minutes

MATERIALS:

20 inches of wire

Polymer clay

Scissors

Cloth

Found objects (feathers, flowers, leaves)

Hot glue gun and glue sticks

There are several symbols and figures people call upon to help them feel protected and comforted. These symbols and figures include spirit guides, angels, archangels, and many others. Creating a doll figure allows you to create a physical symbol of your protector. The doll becomes your symbol for what you desire and want to manifest.

STEPS:

1. To begin, set an intention for your doll. What role do you want this doll to play for you? Is it to help you feel peace, protection, or to be a guide for a journey? Spend 10 minutes thinking about what intention you want to place on this doll. Once you decide, keep this intention in mind the entire time you're creating your doll.

2. Start by cutting your wire into 2 equal pieces.

3. Fold one piece of the wire at the top in half to make a U-shape.

4. Twist the U portion of the wire to create a circle shape. This will be the head of your doll.

5. Wrap the second piece of wire around the middle of the first wire to create 2 arms. The 2 end pieces of your first wire should now be sticking out like legs.

6. Place the polymer clay around the top of the circular wire to form a head.

7. Sculpt a face onto the head.

8. Bake your doll in the oven following the polymer clay package directions.

9. Wrap fabric and found objects around the wire to adorn the body.

10. Use hot glue as needed to hold the fabric and objects in place.

Questions for Discussion:

- What is the intention you set for your doll? Say it aloud.

- Where do you plan to keep your doll?

- What is your doll's name?

- How do you plan to use your doll to continue to manifest your intentions?

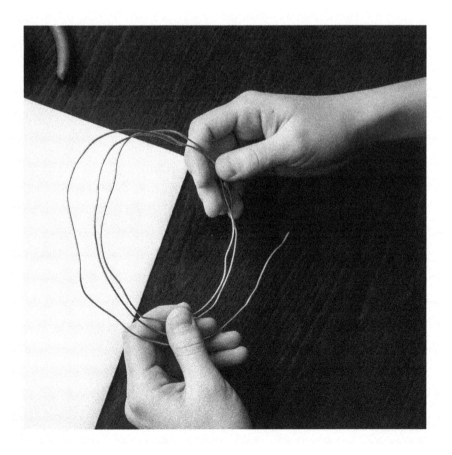

Mask Making

BENEFITS:

Improves self-awareness, emotion regulation, and coping skills

Exercise time:
1 hour

MATERIALS:

Plaster wrap

Scissors

Bowl of water

Face mold

Acrylic paint

Paintbrushes

Cup of water

Mask making is a way to express what we reveal or conceal to the world. The outside of the mask can reflect how we see ourselves or what we show people. The inside of the mask can be a container for our emotions. We may be hiding emotions that are socially unacceptable, such as anger, greed, jealousy, or shame. The mask allows us to express the emotions that we have been repressing. There are two ways to approach this exercise and both sets of directions are listed below. The goal of the first exercise is to add a new coping skill for dealing with strong emotions. The goal of the second exercise is to make your current emotions visible.

STEPS:

1. Cut strips of plaster wrap.

2. Dip the plaster wrap into the water to activate the plaster.

3. Place the strips onto the face mold.

4. Add 3 layers of these strips over the mold in order to make the mask sturdy.

5. Wait 15 minutes for the mask to set and dry.

6. Paint the inside of the mask with the colors you currently feel.

7. **EXERCISE 1:** Think of a new coping skill you would like to master to help you better manage your emotions. Once you have the skill in mind, think of a color that you associate with this skill. Paint the outside of the mask that color.

8. **EXERCISE 2:** Alternatively, create a mental image of what is going on in your mind and associate a color with this image. Paint this color on the outside of your mask. For example, you may be reflecting on a recent trauma, and that trauma is red in your mind. In this case, you would paint the outside of your mask red.

Questions for Discussion:

- Place the mask on your face and play out the role of the character you created. What does this person want to say?

- How is the feeling on the inside of the mask different from what is displayed on the outside?

- What have you learned about yourself?

Grounding Rocks

BENEFITS:

Relieves anxiety and develops coping skills

Prep time:
10 minutes

Exercise time:
30 minutes

MATERIALS:

Small rock (like a river rock)

Assorted markers

Grounding rocks are a great way to help you relieve anxious feelings by grounding your energy. Grounding your energy is an exercise that connects you energetically to the earth. When this happens, you are more present in the moment. A grounding rock is something you can keep in your pocket and hold when you feel overwhelmed. The act of holding the rock in your hand will trigger you to be calm and present. In addition, you can add a word to this process that makes you smile. Other ways to feel grounded include standing barefoot in the grass, touching the trunk of a tree, or taking ten slow, deep breaths.

STEPS:

1. Look through an assortment of river stones about the size of your palm.
2. Pick out a stone that immediately attracts you and feels good in your hand.
3. Look at your markers and pick a color or colors that resonate with you.
4. Color your rock.
5. Choose a positive word that you find calming and write that word on the stone with a black marker.
6. Carry the stone with you.

Questions for Discussion:

- What triggers your anxiety?
- Can you imagine a feeling of calm coming over you and helping you to cope with your anxiety?
- When do you think it would be a good time for you to carry your rock?

Family Sculpture

BENEFIT:

Fosters understanding of family dynamics

Exercise time:

1 hour

MATERIALS:

Self-drying clay

Sculpting tools

Paper

Drawing pencil

Your upbringing shapes your beliefs and your view of the world as an adult. It's important to explore the roles people played in your life in order to gain insight into your family dynamics. Were the relationships significant, supporting, or challenging? To explore the emotional dynamics and roles within your family, you'll make a clay representation of each family member—mother, father, siblings, and any other close or influential family members.

STEPS:

1. Follow the instructions on the package of clay to create one figure for each of the family members who were significant in your life.

2. While creating each figure, make note of the feelings that arise within you. You might want to consider writing them down on paper.

Questions for Discussion:

- What role does each member of your family play? Where do you fit into this dynamic?

- Who is the most supportive?

- In what ways can you nurture your relationships?

- What feelings come up as you think about your family?

Anger Painbody

BENEFITS:

Improves emotional regulation and coping skills

Exercise time:
1 hour

MATERIALS:

Self-drying clay

Sculpting tools

Emotional pain can be highly destructive if not channeled appropriately. Over time, the holding of negative emotions creates a painbody. I first heard about the painbody from Eckhart Tolle. He says that a painbody is created when we keep and hold onto painful life experiences and neglect to let them go. When we hold onto those negative feelings, we create an energy form of that pain in our body. When that happens to us many times over many years, our painbody grows and festers. In order to heal this energy, we must be able to separate ourselves from the emotion. With this exercise, you will create a clay figure that represents your painbody so you can let go of the emotional pain.

STEPS:

1. Use the clay to create a figure. Start with making a ball for the head.
2. Create a rectangle shape for the body.
3. Make 4 long rectangle shapes for arms and legs.
4. Attach the pieces together using sculpting tools.
5. Add features to your clay painbody.
6. Give your painbody a name.

Questions for Discussion:

- The next time you feel anger, stop and name the anger. By separating yourself from the feeling you can make better choices for how to deal with it. When was the last time your anger was triggered?
- How big was your painbody?
- Are you able to sense other people's painbodies now?

Prayer Flags

BENEFITS:

Expresses hope, dreams, and concerns and sets intentions

Exercise time:

1 hour

MATERIALS:

Fabric

Ruler

Scissors

Sewing needle

Thread

Fabric markers

Fabric paints

Paintbrushes

Cup of water

Cord or string

Prayer flags date back thousands of years to Tibet and Buddhism traditions of block-printed squares with Buddhist imagery. They always incorporate the same five colors, and are hung in the same sequence in groups of 10. The colors represent the five basic elements and should always be hung in order from left to right. Blue is the symbol for space, white for air, red for fire, green for water, and yellow for earth. You can dedicate each piece of cloth to something significant to you. Dedications can be for things like healing, love, friendships, self-care, and self-empowerment.

STEPS:

1. Cut fabric into a 5-by-7-inch square.
2. Fold the top down and stich the top down to create a 3-inch sleeve.
3. Use your fabric markers and fabric paint to decorate your flag with colors and symbols that resonate with you.
4. Using your fabric markers, write words on your flag to cement your intentions.
5. Thread the flag onto a cord and let the flag hang down vertically. Hang your flag outside so the breeze will spread your intentions.
6. To continue the healing, you might consider making a flag each day for 10 days to create a full set to thread together on a single cord.

Questions for Discussion:

- What were the intentions you added to your flag?
- Why are these significant to you at this time of your life?

In a Group Setting: Each person should make their flag and then share their intentions with the group.

Dream Box

BENEFIT:

Identifies goals and dreams

Prep time:
10 minutes

Exercise time:
50 minutes

MATERIALS:

Magazines

Scissors

Cardboard box

A dream box is a tool to set intentions for what you want to bring into your life. It's very similar to a vision board! Choose one intention and find images to represent how it would appear visually. Instead of images, you could use a transitional object and store that in the box. A transitional object is something that brings you comfort, especially in unusual or unique situations. For example, I wear a key necklace as my good luck charm. When I'm not wearing it, I like to keep it in my dream box for safekeeping. Get creative in thinking through all of the details of what you want to bring into your life.

STEPS:

1. Take some time to identify one thing you would like to bring into your life.

2. Cut images and positive quotes from magazines to represent that desire and place them in your dream box.

3. Use the box as a holder for a special transitional object that brings you comfort throughout the day (such as a bracelet, charm, or stone).

Questions for Discussion:

- If there were no limitations or fears, what would you wish for?

- Do you believe you are worthy of receiving anything you wish?

- What is stopping you from manifesting this desire now?

- Can you think of an affirmation related to your dream that will build your confidence in making that dream a reality?

Assemblage Art

BENEFITS:

Increases problem-solving skills and provides stress relief

Exercise time:

1 hour

MATERIALS:

Found objects from around your house (small toys, knickknacks, broken items, old jewelry, etc.)

Wooden box (about the size of a cigar box)

Hot glue gun and glue sticks

Assemblage is the art of assembling three-dimensional found objects. It is similar to collage, but collage is only a two-dimensional medium. Composing an arrangement of found objects and creating something new gives those objects a new meaning. You can include personal items that hold precious memories, trinkets from a trip, or random interesting things that catch your eye. Allow the art-making process to unfold and surprise you.

STEPS:

1. Playfully combine objects and fit them into the wooden box.
2. Find ways to make something new out of what is old.
3. Glue the objects together or to the box.
4. Assign new meaning to the work you created.

Questions for Discussion:

- How does your art piece reflect where you are in your life right now?
- Were you surprised with the outcome? Did you find this challenging?
- How did you deal with challenges as they arose?
- What message would your art give you if it could speak?

Tin Full of Hope

BENEFIT:

Relieves anxiety, depression, and PTSD

Prep time:
10 minutes

Exercise time:
1 hour

MATERIALS:

Tin mint box

Spray paint

Found objects

Assorted papers and photos

Hot glue gun and glue sticks

Think about the beauty of a pocket-sized sculpture that holds a powerful message of importance to you. Now let's add hope to that visual image. Hope is the expectation of your desires to manifest. The mindset of healing and creating a fulfilled life should be at the forefront of your beliefs because it is certainly a tangible hope that many share. What does hope look like to you? Is there a symbol, animal, or message that your tin could hold that resonates hope?

STEPS:

1. Take 10 minutes to identify what you want more of in your life.

2. Spray-paint the outside of the tin mint box.

3. Use found objects, papers, and photos to assemble a scene in the mint tin box that represents what you want more of.

4. Glue the scene into the box.

Questions for Discussion:

- What message came to you as you were creating this art?

- Where will you keep your tin box?

- Will it be something you carry with you?

Healing Heart

BENEFITS:

Develops emotional regulation skills and coping skills

Exercise time:
1 hour

MATERIALS:

Fabric (painted or printed)

Scissors

Assortment of found objects, beads, and sequins

Paint

Paintbrushes

Cup of water

Fabric marker

Thread

Sewing needle

Sewing machine (optional)

½ pound of pillow stuffing of your choice

Our hearts are containers for so many emotions. If you could represent the feelings in your heart, what would it look like? Right now, does your heart feel loved, lost, full, free, resentful, broken, heavy, wounded, or light? Our hearts are resilient. With care, attention, and self-compassion you can heal a damaged heart. In this exercise, you are going to create your heart and fill it with what you believe best represents what is inside. I've seen many different types of hearts in my clients' art. Some are broken, one was caged, and others have had wings. Everyone's heart is unique and created by the experiences they have had.

STEPS:

1. Start with painted or printed fabric that is the color of your heart.

2. Cut the fabric into 2 heart-shaped pieces of the same size.

3. Using found objects, beads, sequins, and paint, decorate both pieces of your heart in a way that represents how you see your heart today.

4. With a fabric marker, you can write your story or add a quote to one side of your heart.

5. Once both sides are dry, line up the two hearts back-to-back and sew along the outline of the heart. Be sure to leave a 1-inch gap to insert the stuffing. Insert the stuffing through the hole and sew up the gap.

Questions for Discussion:

- How would you describe your heart today?

- What emotions do you want to carry in your heart into the future?

Memory Threads

BENEFITS:

Increases positive emotions and helps process memories

Prep time:
10 minutes

Exercise time:
50 minutes

MATERIALS:

Memorabilia (ticket stubs, receipts, journal notes, love letters, photographs, pressed flowers, etc.)

Scraps of fabric

Sewing machine (optional)

Sewing needle

Thread

Memory Threads are a collection of your favorite experiences. It's a way to make a piece of art out of your good memories. A special piece like this emphasizes how many precious moments there really are in life. It's important to focus on positive memories because positive and joyful energy attracts more positive and joyful energy. With this exercise, you will gather symbols of positive moments in your life in order to attract more positive experiences. You will be creating something new from past events.

STEPS:

1. Walk around your house and gather memorabilia and scraps of fabric (for example, from a loved one's old shirt) that hold positive energy.

2. Create little bundles of positive memories by wrapping the memorabilia in the scraps of fabric.

3. Use a sewing machine to stitch together the bundles. If you don't have a sewing machine, you can use a needle and thread to pull the pieces together.

4. You can hang your Memory Threads on the wall, if you like, or you can carry them around with you.

Questions for Discussion:

- What feelings came up for you as you collected memories?

- How did you bundle the memories together?

- Does your art piece reflect a certain time in your life?

- What would you like to do now to increase positive feelings?

- Many of my clients like to plan out fun dates for themselves or reconnect with people in order to re-experience happy moments. What could you do to reconnect with yourself or others to recreate happy moments?

Casted Survivors' Hands

BENEFITS:

Processes emotions, increases self-worth, and helps find empowerment through trauma

Prep time:
10 minutes

Exercise time:
50 minutes

MATERIALS:

Alginate (or another type of hand-casting kit)

Plaster

Gloves

Bowl

Acrylic paint

Paintbrushes

Cup of water

Plaster strips (alternative)

Petroleum jelly (alternative)

Hands are expressive and empowering. Explore different ways your hands can tell a story. What stories are told with a fist, two cupped hands, praying hands, or a peace sign? How do your hands represent how you feel now or how you would like to feel? Hand gestures can deliver an expressive and effective message. I had a client who created a cast of her hands open to receive. The cast came out beautifully; you could even see the details of her tiny hairs and veins. She decided to not paint them and let them remain plaster white.

STEPS:

1. Spend 10 minutes trying out different hand poses. Decide which pose of your hands you want to cast.
2. Follow the directions on the packaging to prepare the alginate. (If you do not have alginate, there are two alternatives you could try instead. One is to pour wet plaster into a rubber glove and close the glove with a rubber band. Let this dry overnight and then remove the rubber glove once dry. Or, you could lay plaster strips around your hand. Be sure to cover your hands in petroleum jelly before applying the strips so the plaster does not stick to your skin. Once set, you can take the plaster mold off your hand.)
3. Find a comfortable sitting position and pour the alginate over your hands.
4. Wait 20 minutes for the alginate to set.
5. Slowly pull your hands from the alginate.
6. Mix the plaster (equal parts dry plaster and water).
7. Pour the plaster into the alginate mold.

8. Let set for a day.

9. Carefully peel away the alginate. Make small cuts to prevent breaking the fragile fingers.

10. Leave your creation in its original white plaster state, or decorate your casted hands with paint.

Questions for Discussion:

- What message does your hand hold?

- Would you like to have your hand physically hold something?

- Did you decide to use paint and embellish your casted hands? Why or why not?

Strength Coil Pot

BENEFITS:

Increases relaxation, decreases anxiety, and increases self-esteem

Exercise time:
1 hour

MATERIALS:

Self-drying clay

Acrylic paint

Paintbrushes

Cup of water

Clay is a very grounding and healing material. The intention behind the Strength Coil Pot exercise is to identify a particular strength for each coil created. Once you start thinking of attributes that describe you, your list of strengths will grow. You probably possess more strengths than you think. This is a difficult exercise, and you are brave for trying it. You can add brave to your list! Are you compassionate, empathetic, creative, bold, daring, inquisitive, smart, playful, or passionate? In this project you will create a planting pot from clay. You'll start by creating the base and then build layers using coils. You can use your coil pot as a planter or as a household container.

STEPS:

1. Play with the clay by punching, pounding, and squeezing it.
2. Flatten a piece into a circle to create the base of your pot.
3. Break off a piece of the clay and roll it on the table to make a snake-like coil.
4. Place the coil around the base of your pot.
5. Continue to make coils and place them on top of the previous coil until the pot reaches your desired height.
6. For each coil that you make, identify one of your strengths.
7. After the clay has dried, paint your pot.
8. If this exercise takes longer than 60 minutes because you made a large pot, feel free to finish your pot on another day. You don't have to create the entire pot in one sitting.

Questions for Discussion:

- Were you surprised by how many strengths you possess?

- Are there any characteristics that you would like to possess moving forward?

- Another way to use the pot is to write a difficult situation on paper and then place the paper inside your pot. Are you experiencing any difficulties that you need strength to handle?

Healing Bowl

BENEFIT:

Develops emotional regulation skills and coping skills

Prep time:
10 minutes

Exercise time:
50 minutes

MATERIALS:

Gesso spray

Ceramic bowl

Blow dryer

Large plastic bag

Hammer

Paint

Paintbrushes

Cup of water

Liquid glue

Assorted markers

In Japanese tradition, there is an art form called *kintsugi* where cracks in a broken bowl are filled with gold. Instead of hiding its history, the broken piece is repaired, and the cracks are made beautiful. The message in this art form is that there is beauty in breaking, healing, and transforming. The bowl is symbolic of us, as we are a vessel that holds many things. Sometimes we break emotionally and need to be repaired. In this exercise, you will break a bowl and then repair it. You will fill the bowl with written words on both the inside and the outside as a representation of your essence. (The bowl will not be food safe after you complete this project.)

STEPS:

1. Apply gesso spray to the outside of the ceramic bowl. (You can use an old bowl or pick one up at a thrift store.)

2. Dry it with a blow dryer. Once dry, place the bowl into a plastic bag.

3. Lay the bag on a hard surface, and tap the edges of the bowl with the hammer to break it into a few pieces.

4. Take the broken pieces out of the bag and paint them.

5. Once the paint is dry, put the bowl back together with glue.

6. Choose a marker color that resonates with you and outline the lines of the breaks on the outside of the bowl.

7. Use the marker to write words on the inside of the bowl that express your feelings.

Questions for Discussion:

* Do you feel your difficult experiences have made you more beautiful?

* Have they made you wiser, stronger, or more compassionate?

Acceptance Box

BENEFITS:

Manages emotions and develops coping skills

Exercise time:

50 minutes

MATERIALS:

Small wooden or cardboard box

Acrylic paint

Paintbrushes

Cup of water

Liquid glue

Found objects

Pen

Paper

The Acceptance Box is a container for situations, feelings, or challenges that you cannot control. The box holds your anxieties, fears, insecurities, or anything that is taking up space in your head. Through the process of writing down these worries and mindfully placing them into the box, you give those worries to a higher power to resolve. This is a symbolic way to free yourself of things you cannot change. In doing this, you are accepting the solution knowing you did all you could do. This art experience helps us learn to let go of our anxieties and embrace the experience as a learning journey. I've seen this exercise relieve anxiety in my clients because it gave them the power to choose to no longer worry about a situation.

STEPS:

1. Paint the outside of the box.
2. Use the glue to decorate the box with found objects.
3. Write down any secret, fear, insecurity, or anxiety on a piece of paper and mindfully place the paper into the box.

Questions for Discussion:

- Can you feel a difference when you allow a higher power to take care of your problems?
- Have you previously used faith to manage other life situations?
- Do you use prayer as a way to cope?

Chapter Five

WRITING

IN THE WORLD OF CREATIVE WRITING, feelings can be accessed, pain can be externalized, and experiences can be understood. The exercises found in this chapter are focused on releasing feelings, assessing the self, planning a life, and increasing self-esteem through creative expression. If you feel inspired, you can add imagery, as well. I like to keep a drawing and writing journal as a container for my thoughts and feelings.

Bringing In and Letting Go

BENEFIT:

Identifies what you want to bring into your life and what no longer serves you

Exercise time:
15 minutes

MATERIALS:

Paper

Pen

In this exercise, you will work with a writing prompt that will guide you to become clear on what you want to bring into your life. You are mentally letting go of toxic people, situations, and even objects that no longer serve you. If something is not bringing you joy, it's time to make a change. Many clients find that letting go of clutter in their lives brings relief and helps them feel lighter. Letting go of physical objects can be a great first step.

STEPS:

1. On a piece of paper, draw a line down the middle to create two columns.
2. In the left column, add the heading Bring In.
3. In this column, create a list of all the things you want to bring into your life. This may include people, feelings, experiences, and objects.
4. In the right column, add the heading Let Go.
5. In this column, create a list of all the things in your life that no longer serve you. This may include people, feelings, experiences, and objects.
6. Once your lists are complete, tear off the Let Go side of the paper, rip it into tiny pieces, and throw it away.

Questions for Discussion:

- It's time to take action. Mark on your calendar when you will work on your goals. What will you do to let go of the people, places, or objects in your life that no longer serve you?
- How will you start the process of bringing in the feelings and experiences you would like to have?

Overcoming Fear

BENEFIT:

Increases coping skills

Exercise time:
30 minutes

MATERIALS:

Journal

Pen

Fear serves a purpose that can be necessary for survival. Fear is a natural response for protection. However, when fear and anxiety start to negatively impact our lives, we can become stuck. Fear can stop you from living your best life. This exercise will help you understand how fear is playing a role in your life. Using your nondominant hand for this writing exercise will tap into your unconscious mind.

STEPS:

1. In your journal, use your nondominant hand to make a list of three fears that are interfering with your life.

2. Continue to use your nondominant hand to write responses to these questions:

   - When was the last time you experienced fear?
   - If fear was not present, what life experiences would you be able to have?
   - How is the fear serving you? Is it helping in any way?
   - Where is the fear coming from?
   - What lesson does your fear need to teach you?

Questions for Discussion:

- When fear shows up, ask yourself: Is this real or imagined?

- If the fear is real and you're in danger, immediately seek help. If it is not real, then create an affirmation statement that supports your dreams. A simple statement such as, "I choose love instead of fear," can help you move forward and become unstuck. What are some other affirmations you can think of to help you battle your fear?

Helpful and Harmful Chart

BENEFIT:

Promotes good decision-making and coping skills

Exercise time:
15 minutes

MATERIALS:

Journal

Pen

This exercise provides a visual representation of coping skills. When you realize you have the tools to tackle your feelings of being overwhelmed, stressed, angry, or sad, you feel empowered. We all get stressed—it's how we constructively deal with the stress that's important. This exercise has helped clients realize that they are always supported. It helps them gain control over their emotions.

STEPS:

1. Draw a line down the middle of a journal page and create two columns.

2. In the left column, add the heading Helpful.

3. In the right column, add the heading Harmful.

4. In the Helpful column, create a list of all the helpful strategies you have used to deal with overwhelming emotions (for example, talking to someone, drawing, taking a walk, reading a book, or meditating).

5. In the Harmful column, write down all of the harmful strategies you have used to deal with overwhelming emotions (for example, alcohol, rage, negative self-talk, isolation, or self-harm).

6. As you complete these two columns, it's important that you're honest with yourself so that you can make necessary changes.

Questions for Discussion:

- How have you been responding to overwhelming emotions?

- Avoidance is a strategy to handle emotions that presents itself in many ways. Some of these ways include watching television or not engaging with others, both of which are harmful ways to deal with overwhelming emotions. The underlying uncomfortable feeling is still present. It's important to be proactive in dealing with issues. Have you been using helpful or harmful strategies?

Retelling Your Story

BENEFIT:

Develops decision-making and coping skills

Exercise time:

55 minutes

MATERIALS:

Journal

Pen

Retelling stories can build emotional regulation skills. Revisiting a traumatic event allows you to have an emotional distance and process the memory. Many people with traumatic experiences remember the events in fragments. By piecing the parts of the story together, it helps the brain integrate the memory into the mind. The more times a traumatic event and its impact is discussed, the easier it becomes to deal with the emotions.

STEPS:

1. Recall, reflect, and write about a traumatic event.
2. Recall the experience in detail, including sights, sounds, tastes, and physical sensations. If you can't remember the entire event, it's okay to include only what you remember. If you feel overwhelmed or emotionally triggered, then keep your Strength Shield (page 42) nearby.
3. Reflect on your feelings and thoughts during and after the event.

Questions for Discussion:

- What did you hear, say, or touch during the experience? What were you thinking? What emotions did you feel?
- What physical sensations did you experience?
- How has your life been altered by the experience? What tools are you using to cope with your feelings?

Feeling Poem

BENEFITS:

Increases creative expression, cognition, and emotional regulation

Exercise time:
30 minutes

MATERIALS:

Magazine

Scissors

Bowl

Glue

Journal

The healing power of words has been known since the early Egyptians wrote words on papyrus, dissolved the papyrus in water, and then gave it to the sick as medicine. Poems offer an outlet to express your feelings. This exercise helps bring hidden emotions to the surface in order to explore and heal. This is a fun technique that increases problem-solving skills.

STEPS:

1. Cut at least 10 words (nouns, verbs, and adjectives) from a magazine.
2. Place 10 words in a bowl so you can't read them.
3. Pull five of the words from the bowl.
4. Use the words to create a poem by gluing one word on each line of your journal.

Questions for Discussion:

- What feeling words came up for you?
- How does the poem relate to your life?
- Who would you like to share your poem with?

Word Mandala

BENEFITS:

Develops coping skills and emotional regulation

Exercise time:
30 minutes

MATERIALS:

Magazine

Scissors

Glue

Journal

Colored pencils

In Buddhism, mandalas are geometric figures that represent the universe. Mandala means circle, so you will be placing your words in a circular pattern. Words hold power and emotions. When creating your art, find words that evoke something in you. This exercise helps you find clarity and identify feelings. Knowing how you feel makes it easier to deal with the feelings.

STEPS:

1. Cut out words that denote feelings and emotions from a magazine.
2. Choose words that resonate with you.
3. Glue these words in a circular pattern into your journal.
4. Use the colored pencils to decorate your mandala.

Questions for Discussion:

- Why did you choose the words you chose?
- How are you dealing with the emotions you are currently feeling?
- How can you nurture feelings that you want to attract?

Getting Clear

BENEFITS:

Identifies needs, develops self-awareness, and increases coping skills

Exercise time:
20 minutes

MATERIALS:

Journal

Pen

Take some time to think about what you really value in your life. Do you enjoy spending time with your family and friends, being alone, working, eating well, taking care of your body, taking care of your finances, or having fun? Use the writing prompts to explore your feelings and what is important to you. Many times my clients aren't spending their time on the things that are most important to them, which leads to feeling unfulfilled. This activity helps you identify what is important to you.

STEPS:

1. In your journal, write several sentences to complete each of the following writing prompts:

   - I want . . .
   - I need . . .
   - I hope . . .
   - I expect . . .
   - I fear . . .
   - I wish . . .
   - I am . . .
   - I love . . .

2. Look back at what you wrote and circle what is important to you.

Questions for Discussion:

- How can you take action to balance your time and include everything you want?

- Were you surprised by any of your responses?

- Which response evoked the most emotion?

Lifeline History

BENEFIT:

Develops understanding of the past to create the future

Exercise time:
30 minutes

MATERIALS:

Journal

Pen

Understanding your history provides insight into the current events in your life. For example, if a certain feeling keeps surfacing, the ability to compare how that feeling has shown up in other areas of your life can help you heal. If you could go back to speak to your younger self, what would you say? In this exercise, you will write to your younger self with your nondominant hand. By looking at the past, you can see how you might be carrying unnecessary baggage that is stopping you from moving forward.

STEPS:

1. Draw a line across one page of your journal to create a timeline.
2. On the line, create an outline of dates starting from birth, through childhood and adolescence, to present day.
3. Add significant events in your life such as celebrations, awards, happy times, and sad times.
4. Include significant people and relationships.
5. On the next page of your journal, write the answers to the Questions for Discussion below.

Questions for Discussion:

- How did you respond to certain events?
- Did any particular event make a longstanding impression on you?
- What did you learn about yourself from reviewing your timeline?
- Are you holding any resentment that is keeping you from connecting with people now?

Best Next Step

Assists in problem solving
and decision making

Exercise time:
30 minutes

MATERIALS:

Journal

Pen

Identifying problems and exploring possible response scenarios can help you see different perspectives of a situation. Looking at different outcomes can also help you find a solution. When you're anxious and in fight-or-flight mode, your brain is not responding from a place of healthy problem solving. It's responding from a place of fear. You first need to take some time to calm down. Once you are calmer, you can write out different scenarios to solve your problem.

STEPS:

1. Identify a current problem you are experiencing.
2. Write out three solutions to the problem.
3. Write out the pros and cons to each solution.
4. Consider if there are consequences to each solution.
5. Consider how you think you will feel in each scenario.
6. Review your solutions and choose the best option.
7. This writing exercise can be done as a drawing instead. Be creative and have fun with the process.

Questions for Discussion:

* How did you determine which was the best solution? Did you use logic, gut instinct, or both?

* How did it feel to create a game plan to resolve an issue?

Self-Talk

BENEFITS:

Creates self-awareness, promotes positive thinking, and builds problem-solving skills

Exercise time:
20 minutes

MATERIALS:

Journal

Pen

Negative self-talk feeds depression. When you become aware of this behavior, you can learn to replace negative statements with more positive ones. Is there something you really want out of life? Do you have negative thoughts or beliefs that are associated with getting what you want? I've seen the negative thoughts of one of my clients creep into different areas of her life. She kept telling herself that she wasn't good enough. This affected her relationships at work, at home, and with herself. When she recognized this pattern and replaced her internal dialogue with helpful, positive thoughts, her outlook on life and relationships changed. It will do the same for you.

STEPS:

1. Identify a negative self-statement or thought and write it down in your journal.

2. Write down the opposite phrase. For example, "I hate myself," would become, "I love myself."

3. Repeat this exercise for as many negative self-thoughts you may have.

Questions for Discussion:

- Have you ever noticed how much negative self-talk occurs throughout your day?

- Now that you've taken inventory of your thoughts by writing them down, check back with them in a week. What has changed?

Fill Your Cup

BENEFITS:

Develops self-esteem, self-awareness, and coping skills

Exercise time:
30 minutes

MATERIALS:

Journal

Pen

Many people think of self-care as the maintenance of our physical body; for example, bathing or getting a haircut. Yes, these activities may feel great, but nurturing the inner self is just as important. Our society drives a culture of rushing around, tackling to-do lists, and constantly multitasking. This exercise will help you focus on slowing down. In fact, by reading this book you are already moving in the right direction! How would you like to fill your cup? By nurturing yourself first, you're able to give more to others. If you have a full cup, you have more to share.

STEPS:

1. Draw a large cup in your journal.

2. Write down self-care activities inside your cup. Include activities that you can do to feel good throughout the day. For example, you might include how you like to enjoy a cup of tea, take a bath, play with paint, schedule a therapist appointment, review your goals, buy yourself some flowers, or take a walk.

Questions for Discussion:

- You need to nourish to flourish. How are you taking care of yourself?

- Do you allow yourself time to play, relax, and enjoy the moment?

- What is the first self-nurturing activity you are planning to do? Schedule it!

Embracing Your Strengths

BENEFITS:

Builds self-esteem and self-awareness

Exercise time:
20 minutes

MATERIALS:

Journal

Pen

Everyone has unique experiences in life. Most of these opportunities are unique to you because they embrace one or more of your strengths. One time I got to sit in a four-seater airplane and fly over California. It was a thrilling experience. My openness to adventure allowed me to participate in this encounter. This exercise aims to reprogram your mind into a positive mode. Think about an amazing experience you've had: Was it an adventure or an opportunity? Knowing that you've experienced special events helps you see that life has so much to offer!

STEPS:

1. In your journal, write down one amazing experience that you have had.

2. Next, list all the positive qualities that you possess. Here are some examples of positive qualities:

   - Empathetic
   - Strong
   - Creative
   - Trustworthy
   - Reliable
   - Honest

3. If you feel stuck, reach out to some friends and ask them what qualities they see in you.

4. If there is ever a time when you are feeling challenged in the future, revisit your list.

Questions for Discussion:

- Is there a connection between this experience and your talents?

- Celebrate yourself today. What about you makes you unique?

Visualize It

BENEFIT:

Encourages goal-setting

Exercise time:
30 minutes

MATERIALS:

Journal

Pen

Visualization is a powerful tool that can bring about positive experiences. Through visualization, we can train the brain to make goals and envision a reality. Visualization is often used by athletes and executives so their brains can process their future success as a reality. What is it that you really want in your life? Dream big in order to allow yourself the freedom to create the life you desire and deserve.

STEPS:

1. Find a quiet and comfortable place to sit.
2. Close your eyes.
3. Take a few moments to visualize your ideal day. Be sure to start from the moment you awake and include all of the details in your day.
4. Let your imagination run the show. You might even choose certain feelings that you would like to experience during your ideal day.
5. Once you complete your visualization, write down all the details in your journal.

Questions for Discussion:

- What were the feelings you experienced?
- How can you apply the experiences of your vision to your life today?

Inner Child

BENEFITS:

Develops emotional regulation and coping skills

Exercise time:
30 minutes

MATERIALS:

Journal

Pen

Take some time to connect to your inner child. Think about where you lived and who you spent your time with when you were young. Connecting with your inner child gives you a sense of freedom and reduces the stress you feel as an adult. Think of a child who doesn't have any bills to pay; their only responsibility is to go to school and have fun. However, not all childhoods are fun and easy. Maybe your younger self didn't have a chance to play. In this exercise, you will connect with your preteen identity to promote recognition and healing.

STEPS:

1. Remember yourself as a preteen. What did you like to wear? Who did you pretend to be? What were your favorite things to do, eat, and play?

2. Use your nondominant hand to write a letter from your eight-year-old self to yourself today. What would you like to tell your adult self?

Questions for Discussion:

- What message does your inner child want to tell you?

- Are you giving yourself time to play as an adult?

- If your inner child is in need of healing, what do they want to experience?

I Am Grateful for . . .

BENEFIT:

Improves coping skills

Exercise time:
20 minutes

MATERIALS:

Journal

Pen

Assorted markers

Gratitude is strongly associated with greater happiness. Gratitude changes mindsets and helps people feel more positive emotions. Positive emotions foster a more fulfilling life. You can feel gratitude for even the smallest things, like a cup of coffee or a friendly smile. By practicing gratitude, your mind starts to look for things throughout the day to be grateful for, thus bringing more abundance to your life. This exercise works best if you practice it daily.

STEPS:

1. In your journal write the words, "I am grateful for . . ." and draw a big circle around them.
2. Inside the circle, add the people, places, and things you are grateful for.
3. Use the markers to add color to your creation.

Questions for Discussion:

- Do you feel you have enough support in your life?
- What are you most grateful for today?

Chapter Six

COLLAGES

COLLAGING INCORPORATES A VARIETY OF MATERIALS.
It involves sorting through imagery, cutting, gluing, and assembling
items to create a desired composition. Each art experience will help
you gain insight into different areas of your life.

Life Book

BENEFITS:

Boosts creative expression and identifies goals

Prep time:
5 minutes

Exercise time:
45 minutes per page

MATERIALS:

Old hardcover book

Magazines

Scissors

Glue

The Life Book gives you a holistic overview of your life. Use this book as a personal journal. Each page will be dedicated to a goal you want to accomplish. The Life Book gives you an opportunity to design your life. Each area needs attention. You may want to review your values from Getting Clear (page 111) for ideas. This activity can be done as often as necessary to fill up the book. Dedicate time to work on one page today.

STEPS:

1. Find an old hardcover book that you can repurpose. You will be writing and pasting things inside this book to make your collage.

2. Identify what you value in your life and how you want to spend your time. Dedicate at least one page from the hardbound book to each area of your life: physical, spiritual, mental, emotional, financial, and relational (family, parent, friendships, partner). Write one area at the top of each page.

3. Cut out words and images from the magazines that match how you want to spend your life.

4. Glue these words and images to the pages inside the book.

Questions for Discussion:

* What discoveries did you make about what you want to bring into your life?

* What feelings came about as you were designing your life?

Life Goals Collage

BENEFIT:

Identifies goals

Exercise time:
1 hour

MATERIALS:

1 sheet of 18-by-24-inch
heavy-weight
drawing paper

Drawing pencil

Magazines

Scissors

Glue

It's important to know what you want to improve in your life. The Life Goals Collage can begin the journey to bring what you want into your life. What is it that you desire? Do you want to improve your relationships, your mindset, or how you feel? Gaining clarity on what you want is the first step toward attaining your goals.

STEPS:

1. Divide the piece of paper into three equal parts.
2. For each of the three sections, identify one area in your life you would like to work on. For example, part one could be family, part two could be social life, and part three could be work.
3. Choose three goals in each section that you would like to focus on.
4. Cut out images from the magazines that represent these goals.
5. Glue those images into appropriate sections of your paper to provide visual elements to your goals.

Questions for Discussion:

- What came up for you in the collage?
- How can you take one step today to bring one of your goals into your life?

Life Reflection Collage

BENEFIT:

Improves emotional regulation

Exercise time:
50 minutes

MATERIALS:

Magazines

Scissors

Glue

1 sheet of 18-by-24-inch heavy-weight drawing paper

The Life Reflection Collage will allow you to honor the moment you are experiencing. Choose images that represent your current feelings. Think of this as a mood board. Accepting current feelings is a way to really experience them and release them. Look for objects, places, and colors that express your current mood. You can be creative with where you place each item and how the items interact with one another.

STEPS:

1. Using the magazines, find a headline that matches how you feel today. Cut out the headline.
2. Find and cut out other words that resonate with you today.
3. Find and cut out pictures that reflect your life today.
4. Glue the images onto the paper.

Questions for Discussion:

- What feelings came up for you as you created your current life experience?
- Is there an overall color theme?
- What message does your art have for you?

Anxiety Collage

BENEFITS:

Expresses emotions, improves emotional regulation, and decreases anxiety

Exercise time:

1 hour

MATERIALS:

Magazines

Scissors

Glue

1 sheet of 18-by-24-inch heavy-weight drawing paper

Assorted markers

Everyone experiences some level of anxiety. Anxiety becomes an issue when you feel that you are no longer in control and worry constantly. In this exercise you will explore all of the experiences that provoke anxiety. In order to help relieve the emotion, we need to know what is provoking it.

STEPS:

1. Find magazine images that provoke feelings of anxiety and cut them out.

2. Glue the images onto the paper.

3. Use the markers to write down your thoughts related to the images and situations.

4. Give your collage a name. Think of coping skills that will help you relieve your feelings of anxiety.

5. After completing the collage, it would be helpful to draw a Healing Symbol (page 33) to help ground you.

Questions for Discussion:

- What places trigger your anxiety?

- What feelings come up in your body when you look at your collage?

- Are you willing to let go of the worry and control?

Tissue Paper Collage

BENEFITS:

Increases relaxation and improves problem-solving skills

Exercise time:

50 minutes

MATERIALS:

Tissue paper in assorted colors

Liquid glue

Bowl

Water

Paintbrush

1 sheet of 18-by-24-inch heavy-weight drawing paper

A Tissue Paper Collage is an expressive image. You will be starting out with no intention or direction. Allow yourself to be playful and open to what unfolds. Use colors that resonate with you to create an abstract form. Placing the small colored pieces together to look like stained glass is a meditative practice.

STEPS:

1. Tear sheets of different colored tissue paper into small pieces.

2. Pour liquid glue into a bowl with a small amount of water. Mix the glue and water with the paintbrush. The consistency should be thick, but add more water as needed if mixture becomes difficult to spread.

3. Place the colored tissue paper pieces on the paper to create a design.

4. Dip the paintbrush into the glue mixture and gently paint over the tissue paper so that the pieces adhere to the paper.

Questions for Discussion:

- Did a shape, object, or form appear? If so, what does it mean for you?

- What colors did you use? Why did you choose those colors?

- What feelings came about for you?

Inner-Self/Outer-Self Collage

BENEFIT:

Develops self-awareness

Exercise time:

1 hour

MATERIALS:

Magazines

Scissors

1 sheet of 18-by-24-inch heavy-weight drawing paper

Glue

Self-awareness is conscious knowledge of one's own character, feelings, motives, and desires. True authenticity is being able to share what you feel on the inside with others. In this exercise you will create a visual representation of your inner emotional state and see if it's a match with what others know of you. Are you walking around smiling when you feel sad inside? Do you show others your true self? Viewing your inner and outer self will give you perspective on the emotions you are holding in versus those you are sharing with the people in your life.

STEPS:

1. Cut out words and images of feelings from the magazines. For example, look for images of happiness, joy, sadness, apathy, boredom, anger, rage, frustration, love, shock, anxiety, and disgust.

2. Divide your paper in half.

3. On one side of your paper, place the words and images of the feelings you hold inside.

4. On the other side of the paper, place the words and images of the feelings you share with others.

Questions for Discussion:

- Is there a connection between your feelings and what you share with others?

- Are you able to be vulnerable and share yourself with people?

- Are there parts of yourself that you only share with certain people?

Manifesting Collage

BENEFITS:

Increases self-awareness and identifies strengths

Exercise time:
1 hour

MATERIALS:

Magazines

Scissors

Assorted markers

Glue

1 sheet of 18-by-24-inch heavy-weight drawing paper

Think of strengths that you would like to embrace. Maybe you'd like to be bolder, more adventurous, or healthier? In this exercise, you'll be incorporating these elements into a self-portrait. One of my clients created a sexy, bold, fierce version of herself. She realized afterward that she wasn't showing up in her life with this vitality, yet she craved to nurture this part of herself. She took initiative to be more present in her business and to embrace confidence.

STEPS:

1. Cut out a figure from the magazine to represent the self you desire.
2. Use the markers to change the personal attributes to match your own (eye color, nose, clothes).
3. Glue the figure to the paper.
4. Add words that describe what you want to manifest to the background.
5. Add a colorful border to your collage to give it a finished look.

Questions for Discussion:

- What strengths have you identified that you want to work on?
- What have accepted about yourself?
- How did this process make you feel?
- How will you take this new idea of you into your life?

Safe Place Collage

BENEFITS:

Improves coping skills and decision-making skills

Exercise time:
1 hour

MATERIALS:

Magazines

Scissors

Glue

1 sheet of 18-by-24-inch heavy-weight drawing paper

You can think of this collage as a safety plan. You can also use it as a tool for emotional regulation. When overwhelming emotions appear, view your Safe Place Collage to calm down and relieve anxiety.

STEPS:

1. Choose images from the magazines that bring about a relaxing feeling. You can also choose images of self-care practices for your collage.

2. Cut the images out of the magazines and glue them onto the paper.

3. Hang the collage so you can look at it when you are feeling anxious or depressed.

Questions for Discussion:

* Are there any other items that you would like to add to your image to make you feel safe?

* Are there any barriers, fences, or walls protecting you? If so, what do these images symbolize?

* How would you incorporate your five senses into describing your safe place?

In a Group Setting: If completing this as a group, you can pre-cut the magazine images before you all come together to create your collages.

Accordion Book Collage

BENEFITS:

Develops coping skills and goal-setting skills

Exercise time:
1 hour

MATERIALS:

2 sheets of 8-by-12-inch paper

Tape

Magazines

Scissors

Glue

Paint

Paintbrush

Cup of water

Making the Accordion Book Collage gives you an opportunity to define the areas of your life where you can make changes in order to achieve desired goals. For each collage, I like to choose a single word that will give me some direction in achieving my goals. Recently my word was *effulgent*, which means shining brightly. The theme of your book should be related to your goal. Allow images to come to you that relate to your intention.

STEPS:

1. Tape both sheets of paper together and then fold horizontally in a back and forth motion to create four separate panels.

2. Use the magazines to find images of what you are attracted to and what you want to bring into your life.

3. Choose one word as the theme for your book. Cut out the images that relate to this intention.

4. Glue the images onto the pages of your book. You can also use the front and back of the book.

5. Use paint to fill in the extra white space and decorate your book.

Questions for Discussion:

* What are a few goals that you can accomplish that match what you have placed in your collage?

* What was your word? What activities can you do to bring this word to life?

Fear Collage

BENEFITS:

Processes feelings and improves emotional regulation, decision-making, and coping skills

Prep time:
10 minutes

Exercise time:
50 minutes

MATERIALS:

Magazines

Scissors

Glue

1 sheet of 18-by-24-inch heavy-weight drawing paper

Acrylic paint

Paintbrushes

Cup of water

While you're processing a traumatic event or feeling depressed, fear might keep you from feeling motivated to practice self-care. Fear can be overwhelming and can stop you from moving forward. Some fears are good because they can prevent you from being hurt. But some fears are illusions that stop you from progressing through life. This exercise identifies your fears and helps you regulate your emotions about them.

STEPS:

1. Take 10 minutes to identify three fears that are stopping you from being happy or achieving your goals.
2. Choose images from the magazines that represent your fear.
3. Cut out the images and glue them to your paper.
4. Once all three fears have been represented, choose the paint colors that represent your fear and add these colors to your collage.

Questions for Discussion:

- Are your fears based on physical threats or psychological threats?
- Can you think of any positive self-statements that will address your fears?

Needs Collage

BENEFITS:

Identifies emotional needs and improves decision making

Exercise time:
1 hour

MATERIALS:

1 sheet of 18-by-24-inch heavy-weight drawing paper

Assorted markers

Computer

Printer

Scissors

Glue

We all have basic needs that require nurturing. This collage gives you a framework to see which needs are being addressed and which ones need attention. If you aren't getting your needs met, you will feel off balance or that you are missing something in your life. You can make better choices when you can see and address each need. If a particular area needs attention, schedule some time in the next few days to focus your energy on this area.

STEPS:

1. Split your paper into seven columns.

2. Label each column as follows:

   - Safety needs (reasonable protection from psychological and physical harm)
   - Physical needs (food, shelter, water)
   - Control needs (power and influence on situations)
   - Trust needs (good relationships)
   - Self-esteem needs (how you feel about yourself)
   - Personal enjoyment needs (doing things for fun)
   - Personal growth needs (spirituality and community connection)

3. Choose images from the Internet that represent each category.

4. Print those images.

5. Cut the images out and glue them into the correct category.

6. Feel free to be creative and add your own designs to the page with your markers.

Questions for Discussion:

- Are your self-care needs balanced?

- Is there an area that needs attention?

Guilt and Shame Collage

BENEFIT:

Releases emotions

Exercise time:

1 hour

MATERIALS:

Magazines

Scissors

Glue

1 sheet of 18-by-24-inch
heavy-weight
drawing paper

Assorted markers

Watercolors

Paintbrush

Cup of water

Guilt is feeling that you are responsible for a wrongdoing. Even if you apologize the feeling may linger. Shame is an even more painful feeling of humiliation. Shame can lead a person to think they are unworthy of love, friendships, or happiness. It can affect unrelated areas of your life and lead to isolation, dishonesty, abusive behaviors, alcoholism, or workaholism. Many people who have shame are too embarrassed to get help, but it's important to identify when the feelings of shame started. Discussing your work with a trained therapist can help you share your story and begin the healing process.

STEPS:

1. Choose images from magazines that represent guilt and shame. Cut them out.

2. Glue the images onto the paper.

3. Using the markers, add words that express your feelings.

4. Use the watercolors to add color to your collage.

Questions for Discussion:

- How did you feel creating this collage?

- Have you been able to forgive yourself and others involved?

- What message does your art have for you?

All in Your Head Collage

BENEFITS:

Develops coping skills,
identifies feelings,
increases self-awareness

Exercise time:
1 hour

MATERIALS:

Magazines

Scissors

Glue

1 sheet of 18-by-24-inch
heavy-weight
drawing paper

Assorted markers

Sometimes you don't realize how busy you are and how full your mind is. Creating a visual representation of the thoughts that exist in your head will allow you to take a deeper look into what has been occupying your mind. This activity is a great way to assess healthy thoughts versus unhealthy ones.

STEPS:

1. Choose an image from a magazine to represent yourself. Cut it out.

2. Glue the image onto the paper.

3. Use the markers to surround the image with lines and designs that illustrate the thoughts in your head.

Questions for Discussion:

- What thoughts take up most of your time?

- Are there any thoughts that are not serving you?

"I AM" Collage

BENEFITS:

Increases self-esteem and
coping skills

Exercise time:

1 hour

MATERIALS:

Pen

1 sheet of 18-by-24-inch
heavy-weight
drawing paper

Magazines

Scissors

Glue

Identifying all your strengths and unique qualities can be incredibly empowering. This collage presents an opportunity to tap into your greatness and realize all the unique things that make you one of a kind. Many of my clients really enjoy this activity because it elevates their mood almost immediately.

STEPS:

1. Write I AM in the center of the paper.
2. Look in the magazines for words that represent all your positive attributes. Cut them out.
3. Glue the words on to the paper radiating out from the words I AM.
4. Keep this image where you will see it often to increase your self-esteem.

Questions for Discussion:

- How does it feel to have all these strengths?
- How can you use these attributes in different areas of your life?

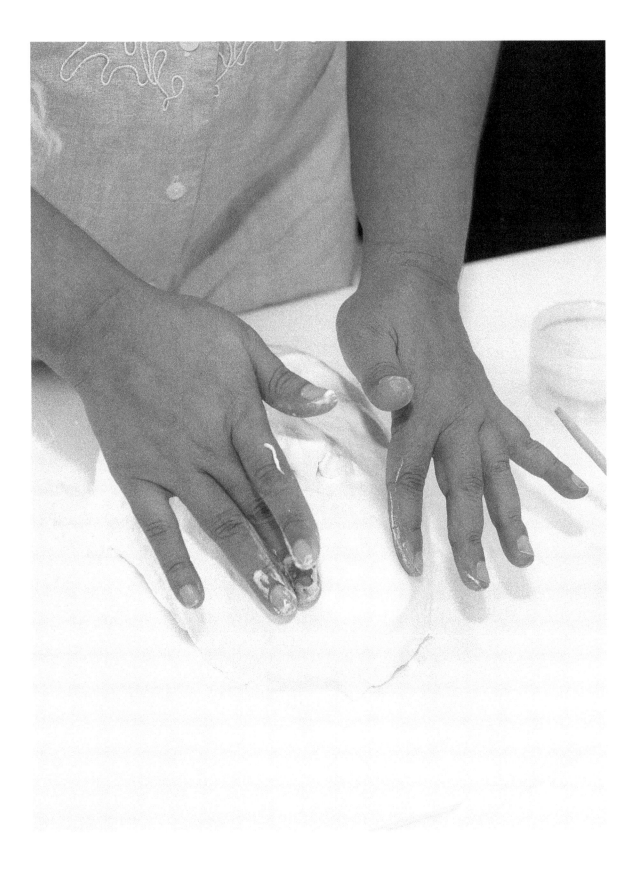

RESOURCES

For more information about art therapy:

American Art Therapy Association:
www.arttherapy.org

Author's website:
www.leahguzman.com

Psychology Today:
www.psychologytoday.com

Find art materials at these locations:

Blick Art Materials:
www.dickblick.com

Jerry's Artarama:
www.jerrysartarama.com

Crisis telephone numbers in the United States:

American Association of Poison Control Centers:
1-800-222-1222

Crisis Text Line:
Text "DESERVE" TO 741-741

Emergency:
911

Family Violence Helpline:
1-800-996-6228

GLBT Hotline:
1-888-843-4564

Lifeline Crisis Chat (online live messaging):
https://suicidepreventionlifeline.org/chat/

National Council on Alcoholism and Drug Dependence Hope Line:
1-800-622-2255

National Crisis Line—Anorexia and Bulimia:
1-800-233-4357

National Crisis Line:
1-800-999-9999

National Domestic Violence Hotline:
1- 800-799-7233

National Hopeline Network:
1-800-SUICIDE (800-784-2433)

National Suicide Prevention Lifeline:
1-800-273-TALK (8255)

Planned Parenthood Hotline:
1-800-230-PLAN (7526)

Self-Harm Hotline:
1-800-DONT CUT (1-800-366-8288)

REFERENCES

Art Therapy Journal. "The History of Art Therapy." Accessed November 14, 2019. www.arttherapyjournal.org/art-therapy-history.html

GoodTherapy. "Art Therapy." Accessed November 14, 2019. www.goodtherapy.org/learn-about-therapy/types/art-therapy.

Kaimal, Girija, Kendra Ray, and Juan Muniz. "Reduction of Cortisol Levels and Participants' Responses Following Art Making." *Art Therapy* 33, 2 (2016): 74–80. www.ncbi.nlm.nih.gov/pmc/articles/PMC5004743/

National Institute of Mental Health. Accessed November 14, 2019. www.nimh.nih.gov/health/topics/depression/index.shtml

Rosal, Marcia L. *Cognitive-Behavioral Art Therapy*. New York: Routledge, 2018.

Tolle, Eckhart. *A New Earth: Awakening to Your Life's Purpose*. New York: Penguin Books, 2005.

UCLA Mindful Awareness Research Center. Accessed November 14, 2019. www.uclahealth.org/marc/research

INDEX

ACKNOWLEDGMENTS

I would like to acknowledge every professor, mentor, and colleague who has assisted me in my art therapy practice. Thank you to Marcia Rosal, David Gussak, and Betty Jo Traeger for teaching me the foundations. I'm grateful for the opportunity to offer art therapy services to at-risk youth in the Miami-Dade County Public School System. I'm appreciative of my clients for allowing me to be a guiding light. A big shout out to my husband, Jorge Guzman, for his unwavering support in my endeavors.

ABOUT THE AUTHOR

LEAH GUZMAN, ATR-BC, is a board-certified art therapist and professional artist who attained her bachelor of fine arts with an emphasis in sculpture from Georgia State University. She then went on to complete her master's in art education with an emphasis on art therapy from Florida State University. Additionally, while living in California, she attended the San Francisco Art Institute as a transient student.

She has been practicing art psychotherapy in South Florida for 17 years, working in schools, hospitals, crisis shelters, retirement homes, and a juvenile jail. Currently, she provides online art therapy sessions treating patients for anxiety and depression. She also offers full-time clinical services in public schools. Her mission is to offer the gift of creativity for healing in order for others to manifest their most authentic self and best life.

Leah's mixed media paintings are contemporary, symbolic, spiritual in nature, and collected internationally. The multi-genre collection incorporates abstract paintings, figurative work, and the signature interactive installation labyrinths. In her research practicing art therapy and seeing which colors resonate with a person's psychological state, she's recognized the profound power of visual art's essential building blocks.

Printed in the USA
CPSIA information can be obtained
at www.ICGtesting.com
CBHW050333310524
9306CB00009B/107